KAREN MARTINI
Home

KAREN MARTINI
Home

plum. Pan Macmillan Australia

CONTENTS

INTRODUCTION 6
COOK'S NOTES 8

BREAKFAST 10
LUNCHES, SNACKS and **STARTERS** 32
SOUP 56
SALADS and **VEGETABLES** 72
PASTA and **RICE** 110
FISH and **SEAFOOD** 128
CHICKEN 146
MEAT 166
DESSERTS 192
CAKES, BISCUITS and **SWEET TREATS** 214
CHRISTMAS 244

THANK YOU 272
INDEX 275

INTRODUCTION

I've happily spent a big portion of my life in kitchens. From loitering around the family kitchen as a little girl, pestering my mother or grandmother as they cooked, to running service for a dining room full of paying guests. I've worked manic shifts in aging restaurant kitchens, and run brand new ones with a brigade of white-jacketed chefs busily working around me. Somehow, even with a chef's demanding work schedule, I've also always managed to cook enthusiastically at home. Always toyed with ideas, tested technique and played with unusual ingredients and different cuisines. And as time has passed, especially with two young girls to care for, my home kitchen has taken on even more importance. As well as a test kitchen and the engine room for my newspaper, website and book shoots, my kitchen is at the centre of a very busy family life, sustaining, entertaining, surprising and hopefully delighting family and friends.

I love the rigour of a restaurant kitchen, but I also love the freedom of cooking at home. The demands of a restaurant slip away, consistency gives way to variety, and favourite recipes are tweaked and twisted into tasty new versions. At home I'm not bound by a menu or style, I can cook a Thai, Chinese or Spanish dish if I like, and no, it doesn't have to be completely authentic, so long as it's delicious. I might spend five minutes in the kitchen whipping up a quick snack, or hours braising, roasting or baking for a special dinner (or just because I feel like it). Sometimes, when family or friends turn to me with requests, my kitchen goes into full catering mode, and sometimes surprising a loved one with a special plate or homemade sweet treat can be the most personal gift I can give.

When I can, I like to shop every couple of days, picking up fresh produce to supplement a well-stocked pantry, vigorous herb garden and slightly more modest vegetable patch. Like me, my family loves variety and a little bit of intentional over-catering means we'll often have tasty snacks to hand. A bowl of soup is never hard to come by, and there's often a hunk of spanakopita to be had, or perhaps a slice of spiced meatloaf wedged into a baguette with a good smear of chutney. I'll sometimes cure a big piece of ocean trout or marinate a batch of olives, which are actually really easy things to prepare, but just so beautiful to have on hand. Making nutritious food is so important, but food will never simply be fuel to me. Even if I'm rushing out the door and just want something healthy to keep the hunger at bay, I always want that bite to be pleasurable, no matter how simple it is.

This book is about sharing the diversity of my home cooking through the dishes that I love to cook all the time, from the simple and nourishing to the detailed and indulgent. There are solutions to midweek dinner dilemmas, as well as knockout dishes for that special dinner party; super-quick breakfast fixes as well as stylish brunch dishes; light lunches and plenty of plates for the shared table; nourishing wintery soups and vibrant summer ones; some of my current favourite pasta and rice dishes; plenty of exciting meat, chicken and seafood recipes; and delicious sweet treats, from simple biscuits to my all-time favourite pavlova recipe. I seriously celebrate salads and vegetables in this book, as I do at home, and have included a whole chapter devoted to Christmas. Eleven impressive and achievable recipes, from appetiser to dessert, perfect for Christmas or any other time of year.

Cook, eat and enjoy,

Karen Martini

COOK'S NOTES

I always encourage people to read any recipe thoroughly before attempting it. Having an understanding of the method gives you such a head start and takes out any tricky surprises.

CREAM
Unless otherwise stated, cream used in these recipes has a fat content of 35 per cent.

EGGS
Specific egg weights are listed where an accurate quantity is critical to the success of a recipe. When I refer to extra-large eggs I mean an approximate weight of 60–65 g each. I also use extra-large eggs in my savoury recipes, and though they are usually not specified in the ingredients and not critical to success, you will achieve the best results by using them too. I always, at a minimum, use genuine free-range eggs and prefer to use organic eggs whenever possible.

POULTRY AND MEAT
I always buy genuine free-range poultry and pork, and prefer to use organic whenever possible. In almost all instances I prefer grass-fed beef, and like to use dry-aged meat for steaks.

OLIVE OIL
I typically use Australian extra virgin olive oil for most of my cooking. It is more expensive than generic olive oil, but if you buy in larger quantities the cost is dramatically reduced. Extra virgin oil may seem to be lost in a dish when you're sautéing at the start of a braise or the like, but I always like to build flavour and skimping on oil quality will only impact, albeit subtly, on the finished dish. I'm not encouraging you to use a special bottle of peppery oil for frying, just good-quality oil. Extra virgin is also the purest and healthiest olive oil. Olive oils labelled extra virgin and virgin are naturally produced, other olive oils have been refined to make them appropriate for human consumption.

STOCK

I use homemade stock whenever possible. If I have to use a commercial stock, I always use the best that I can find. Simply put, a poor stock will ruin your dish. Many commonly available stocks are sweetened, which is pretty unpalatable to start with, but as soon as the stock is reduced and the sugar (and often added salt) concentrated, it becomes disastrous. Even the best cooks can't bring this one back from the brink. Making a chicken stock from fresh bones or wings is really easy and very economical. It's also a really versatile stock and freezes well.

MAYONNAISE

Although good commercial mayonnaise is readily available, making it is so simple and quick that there is really no need to buy it. Simply whisk an egg yolk with a little mustard and salt until combined. Then slowly add a neutral oil (such as grape seed or rice bran) in a thin stream, whisking constantly, until you have a thick emulsion – one yolk will take up approximately 150 ml of oil. A heavy bowl and an oil bottle with a pourer will make this process easier (or use a hand-held blender). Adjust the mayonnaise with lemon juice or vinegar, and a little salt if needed. It is also recommended, though not essential, that you use room temperature eggs. The key is to add the oil slowly at the start, but once you have an emulsion less care is required. Use as is, or flavour with herbs, saffron, roast garlic, chilli paste, harissa, cornichons, capers or anything else that takes your fancy.

BREAKFAST

- SPICED APRICOT COMPOTE WITH ORANGE BLOSSOM LABNA 12
- TOASTED MUESLI 14
- KALE, BANANA & COCONUT SMOOTHIE 17
- FLUFFY GOAT'S CHEESE & PEA SHOOT OMELETTE 18
- GRILLED MUSHROOMS WITH HALOUMI, CURRANTS, TAHINI & MINT 20
- SHAKSHUKA 23
- SCRAMBLED CURRIED TOFU WITH SPINACH & PEAS 24
- BAKED EGGS WITH RATATOUILLE, RICOTTA & WHITE ANCHOVIES 26
- CORN & CHEDDAR FRITTERS WITH AVOCADO, CORIANDER & CUMIN SALT 29
- VINAIGRETTE POTATOES WITH CORNICHONS, CRÈME FRAÎCHE, FRIED EGG & CORNED BEEF 30

SPICED APRICOT COMPOTE WITH ORANGE BLOSSOM LABNA

I have a real thing for apricots, and when they're not in season (which is most of the time) this is one of my favourite ways to enjoy the dried version. Delicious with muesli or porridge, or you could even use the compote in an upside-down cake, tart or crumble.

Line a colander with muslin or a clean chux cloth, spoon in the yoghurt and fold the fabric over the top. Place the colander over a bowl and refrigerate overnight. The excess whey will drain off the yoghurt, leaving you with thick and creamy labna. When ready to serve, mix the orange blossom water through the labna until combined.

Soak the apricots in boiling water for 30 minutes and drain.

Bring 300 ml of water, the lemon zest and juice, sugar, cardamom pods and cinnamon to a simmer in a medium saucepan. Simmer gently for a couple of minutes to infuse, then add the drained apricots, bring back to a simmer and take off the heat. Serve the compote warm or chilled, with labna and Toasted Muesli (see page 14).

SERVES 4

500 g thick plain yoghurt
2 teaspoons orange blossom water
300 g Australian dried apricots
peeled zest and juice of 1 lemon
120 g caster sugar
4 green cardamom pods, cracked open
2 cinnamon sticks

TIP
This homemade labna also goes well with lots of savoury dishes – sprinkle the labna with dukkah or sumac and eat with flatbread and pickles as mezze; smear it on grilled bread with extra virgin olive oil, roasted peppers, olive paste and ham; or spread it on a platter and drop on hot grilled lamb chops with spring vegetables and soft herbs.

TOASTED MUESLI

This muesli is perfect for me, one that I'm happy to eat every day. It's full of flavour and loaded with healthy seeds and nuts that clump into deliciously crunchy clusters. A handful with thick plain yoghurt and fresh berries is a great way to start the day.

Preheat the oven to 170°C fan-forced (190°C conventional). Line two large baking trays with baking paper.

Mix all of the dry ingredients in a large bowl until combined.

Add the coconut oil, golden syrup and treacle to a small saucepan, warm gently and stir until loosened and combined. Pour the syrup mix into the dry mix and rub through with your fingers, being sure to thoroughly coat.

Spread the mix out in thin layers on the prepared trays and place in the oven for 25 minutes, giving the trays a shake after 10 minutes so that the mix toasts evenly.

Set aside to cool on the trays. The muesli will keep for up to a month in an airtight container.

MAKES 1.5 KG

400 g rolled oats
50 g flaked almonds
100 g whole raw almonds
150 g sunflower seeds
150 g sesame seeds
50 g chia seeds
125 g pumpkin seeds
100 g shredded coconut
100 g sultanas
100 g mixed dried berries (optional)
2½ teaspoons ground cinnamon
1 whole nutmeg, finely grated
100 ml coconut oil (if in a solid state, warm gently to melt)
125 ml golden syrup
125 ml black treacle (or maple syrup)

KALE, BANANA & COCONUT SMOOTHIE

This is such a quick and healthy breakfast. It only takes a few minutes to put together and is light on the mess – there's no need to skip breakfast again.

Place the bananas, kale, coconut water, yoghurt, honey, flaxseed oil, protein powder and ice cubes in a blender or the bowl of a food processor and blitz until smooth. Grate in some fresh nutmeg to taste, blend again and serve.

SERVES 2 GENEROUSLY

2 ripe bananas, peeled
2 handfuls of baby kale (if using more mature kale, strip the leaves from the stalks and shred)
300 ml coconut water
3 heaped tablespoons plain yoghurt
1 tablespoon honey
2 teaspoons flaxseed oil
2 tablespoons protein powder
6 ice cubes
1 whole nutmeg

FLUFFY GOAT'S CHEESE & PEA SHOOT OMELETTE

This is a bit of a show-off breakfast or brunch dish. The light soufflé-like texture is a perfect complement to the soft goat's cheese, while the chives and pea shoots add a fresh lift. Eat this as soon as it comes out of the oven.

Preheat the oven to 180°C fan-forced (200°C conventional).

In a large bowl, whisk the egg whites with a pinch of salt until they form stiff peaks.

In a separate bowl, mix the yolks with some pepper. Gently fold the yolks through the whites until combined.

Heat a splash of oil in a non-stick frying pan over medium–high heat. Pour in the egg mixture, crumble over the goat's cheese, sprinkle with the grated cheese and chives and cook for 2 minutes. Transfer the pan to the oven and bake for 5–8 minutes, or until the omelette is puffed but still has a slight wobble.

Remove from the oven and slide onto a plate, scatter over the pea shoots and peas and serve immediately.

SERVES 2–3

6 eggs, separated
salt flakes and freshly ground black pepper
extra virgin olive oil
100 g soft goat's cheese
50 g gruyere or cheddar, grated
¼ bunch of chives, snipped
1 handful of pea shoots
1 handful of frozen peas, thawed under running hot water

GRILLED MUSHROOMS WITH HALOUMI, CURRANTS, TAHINI & MINT

I made this one morning when I needed a break from regular breakfast fare, and it's become a bit of a favourite. This stands alone as a tasty vegetarian breakfast, but you could always add an egg, and even some bacon if that's your thing.

Preheat the griller.

Place the mushrooms on a baking tray and season with salt and pepper, finely grate the garlic onto the gills and drizzle with oil. Grill for 6–8 minutes until cooked and place on your serving plates.

Heat a frying pan over medium–high heat, add a dash of oil and sear the haloumi on both sides until golden. Place the cooked haloumi on top of the mushrooms.

Mix the lemon juice, tahini and 1 tablespoon of water with a splash of oil until well combined. Spoon the dressing over the mushrooms, scatter over the currants and mint and serve.

SERVES 2

4 large portobello mushrooms, cleaned and stalks trimmed
salt flakes and freshly ground black pepper
2 small garlic cloves
extra virgin olive oil
4 thick slices of haloumi
juice of ½ lemon
1 tablespoon tahini
1 tablespoon currants, soaked in boiling water for 2 minutes and drained
1 handful of mint leaves

SHAKSHUKA

Shakshuka is a classic North African dish of eggs cooked in a spicy tomato-based sauce. Serve with chunks of fresh or toasted pide.

Place the eggs in a large bowl and fill with hot water (warming the eggs will make them cook more quickly).

Heat a large, deep-sided frying pan over medium heat, add a splash of oil and the onion and garlic, stir and cook for 3 minutes. Add the capsicum and cook for 10 minutes, stirring frequently. Add the chilli powder, cumin and paprika and stir through quickly. Stir through the tomatoes, tomato paste, and a splash of water, season and simmer for 10–15 minutes. Adjust the seasoning if necessary and add a pinch of sugar if the tomatoes are too acidic.

Once cooked, make indentations in the sauce around the edge of the pan with a spoon, cracking in the eggs as you go, with one in the centre. Season the eggs, turn the heat down to low and cook for 10–12 minutes, or until the eggs are cooked to your liking. Scatter over the chopped parsley and serve with toasted flatbread.

SERVES 4

8 eggs
extra virgin olive oil
½ white onion, finely diced
3 garlic cloves, finely chopped
2 red capsicums, cut into 2-cm squares
1 yellow capsicum, cut into 2-cm squares
1 teaspoon mild chilli powder
1 teaspoon ground cumin
1 teaspoon smoked paprika
2 × 400 g cans diced tomatoes
3 tablespoons tomato paste
salt flakes and freshly ground black pepper
1 pinch of sugar (optional)
1 handful of flat-leaf parsley leaves, chopped
flatbread, to serve

SCRAMBLED CURRIED TOFU WITH SPINACH & PEAS

Tofu is such a great vehicle for flavour, so make sure you use a good-quality curry powder for this. That's right, not all curry powders are created equal! Look for a fresh one with plenty of aromatic lift.

Add a splash of oil and the garlic to a frying pan over high heat, stir and cook for about 20 seconds until fragrant. Add the curry powder and fry for 10 seconds. Crumble the tofu into the pan, stir through to break it into chunks and cook for 3 minutes. Add the spinach, peas and tamari to the pan and stir through. Cover and cook for a further 2 minutes, or until the spinach has wilted. Tear in the mint leaves and serve with warmed mountain bread.

SERVES 2

extra virgin olive oil
2 garlic cloves, finely grated
1½ teaspoons curry powder
200 g firm tofu
2 big handfuls of baby spinach
½ cup frozen peas
1½ tablespoons tamari
1 handful of mint leaves
2 sheets of mountain bread, warmed

BAKED EGGS WITH RATATOUILLE, RICOTTA & WHITE ANCHOVIES

This is the perfect breakfast dish when you have some ratatouille left over. You could easily use goat's curd or feta instead of ricotta, and salted anchovies would work just as well as white. In summer, try spooning on a little pesto just before serving.

Preheat the oven to 200°C fan-forced (220°C conventional) with the oven grill on.

Heat the ratatouille in a saucepan and, once hot, divide between four small ovenproof ceramic or terracotta dishes. Make indentations in the ratatouille with a spoon and crack in the eggs, season lightly, crumble over the ricotta and lay the anchovies over the top.

Place the dishes in the oven for 10 minutes, or until the eggs are cooked to your liking. Sprinkle with some oregano leaves (if using) and serve.

SERVES 4

½ quantity of Ratatouille (see page 109)
4 eggs, at room temperature
salt flakes and freshly ground black pepper
150 g fresh ricotta
8 premium-quality white anchovy fillets
1 handful of oregano leaves, to serve (optional)
toasted sourdough, to serve

CORN & CHEDDAR FRITTERS WITH AVOCADO, CORIANDER & CUMIN SALT

I love these fritters with bacon, a fried egg and a good spike of green chilli sauce. They're perfect for a weekend brunch, or that late holiday breakfast after a morning swim, with nothing but a lazy day ahead.

For the cumin salt, toast the cumin seeds in a dry frying pan until fragrant, tip into a mortar with the salt flakes and grind to a rough powder.

Sift the cornflour, plain flour and baking powder into a large bowl. Stir in the salt and sugar and make a well in the centre.

In a separate bowl, combine the eggs and milk. Gradually whisk the egg mixture into the dry ingredients until you have a stiff but smooth batter.

Mix the corn kernels, cheese, spring onion and parsley together in a large bowl and season with salt and pepper, pour in the batter and combine.

Heat 2 tablespoons of vegetable oil in a non-stick frying pan over medium heat. When hot, add 2 heaped tablespoons of batter per fritter and cook, in batches of 3–4 fritters at a time, for 2 minutes on each side, or until golden. Repeat, adding more oil as needed.

To serve, mix the avocado with the lime juice, coriander and chilli, season with some cumin salt and serve with the fritters and an extra dusting of cumin salt.

MAKES APPROXIMATELY 10 LARGE FRITTERS

50 g cornflour
200 g plain flour
1 teaspoon baking powder
¼ teaspoon salt flakes, plus extra
1 tablespoon caster sugar
2 eggs
130 ml milk
6 corn cobs, kernels stripped
100 g cheddar, coarsely grated
2 spring onions, sliced
¼ bunch of flat-leaf parsley, leaves picked and chopped
freshly ground black pepper
extra virgin olive oil
2 large avocados, cut into 2-cm dice
juice of 2 limes
1 handful of coriander leaves
1 long green chilli, sliced

CUMIN SALT
1 tablespoon cumin seeds
2 tablespoons salt flakes

VINAIGRETTE POTATOES WITH CORNICHONS, CRÈME FRAÎCHE, FRIED EGG & CORNED BEEF

This is a refined version of a brunch dish I had in the States a couple of years ago. I love the vinegary lift of the potatoes, cornichons and caperberries against the richness of the egg and corned beef. If you're someone who likes to entertain in the morning, this dish is for you.

Boil the potatoes in plenty of salted water until very tender. Drain well, slice in half and add to a large bowl with the vinegar and 2 tablespoons of oil, season with salt and pepper and toss through gently. Set aside for 5–10 minutes to absorb the vinaigrette and cool a little.

Heat a little oil in a non-stick frying pan, crack in the eggs, season and fry until the whites are set but the yolks are still runny.

While the eggs cook, gently toss the cooled potatoes with the parsley, dill, cornichons, spring onion and chilli.

To serve, place the potatoes on your plates, tuck in the corned beef, top with the eggs and caperberries, dollop on the crème fraîche and serve immediately.

SERVES 4

10 chat potatoes, skin on
2 tablespoons white wine vinegar
extra virgin olive oil
salt flakes and freshly ground black pepper
4 eggs
2 handfuls of flat-leaf parsley leaves, torn
1 handful of dill fronds, torn
10 tiny cornichons, cut in half lengthways
2 spring onions, finely sliced
2 long green chillies, finely sliced
12 thin slices of cooked corned beef (you could also use pastrami, smoked trout, gravlax or even bacon)
8 caperberries, cut in half lengthways
4 tablespoons crème fraîche

LUNCHES, SNACKS and STARTERS

MARINATED OLIVES WITH ORANGE, CINNAMON & CHILLI 34

PRESSED CHICKEN & PRUNE TERRINE WITH APPLE, CELERY & WATERCRESS 37

PICKLED BABY OCTOPUS WITH RED WINE, TOMATO & OREGANO 38

SPICED SPINACH, YOGHURT & PINE NUT DIP 41

ROASTED BEETROOT, CINNAMON & POMEGRANATE DIP 41

PITA BREAD 42

FOCACCIA WITH RED ONION, ROSEMARY, OLIVES & CHILLI 44

POTATO CHIP TORTILLA WITH SRIRACHA MAYONNAISE 47

CHICKEN, PRAWN & SHIITAKE POT-STICKER DUMPLINGS 48

ROAST DUCK, MUSHROOM & CORIANDER RICE PAPER ROLLS 50

PRAWN BAGUETTE WITH MINTED CABBAGE & SUMAC 53

FILO PIE WITH GREENS, RICOTTA & PUMPKIN SEEDS 54

MARINATED OLIVES WITH ORANGE, CINNAMON & CHILLI

This certainly isn't a traditional marinade, but orange and cinnamon are great friends and they add such a generously warming perfume to the olives.

Add the olive and vegetable oils to a large saucepan and warm through on a very low heat. Add the orange zest, bay leaves, thyme, chilli, garlic, coriander seeds, cinnamon and about 20 grinds of black pepper and gently warm for 15 minutes to infuse the oil. Add the olives to the pot and warm through.

Tip the olives, oil and aromatics into a large jar and refrigerate. Allow the flavours to properly infuse for 2 days before using.

The olives will keep for up to 2 months in the fridge, simply warm through before serving.

MAKES 1 LARGE JAR

300 ml extra virgin olive oil
300 ml vegetable oil
peeled zest of 1 large orange
4 fresh bay leaves
6 thyme sprigs
4 small red chillies, split lengthways
6 garlic cloves, smashed, skin on
1 tablespoon coriander seeds
2 cinnamon sticks, split
freshly ground black pepper
400 g green olives
400 g black olives

PRESSED CHICKEN & PRUNE TERRINE WITH APPLE, CELERY & WATERCRESS

Making a terrine can often seem a daunting task, but this one is really so simple. Using chicken thighs is the key; they're full of flavour and have enough natural gelatine to bind the terrine perfectly. It's important to use the best chicken you can find – genuine free-range, of course, organic if possible.

You will need a 1.5-litre cast iron terrine mould for this recipe. You also need to prepare the terrine a day before serving.

Preheat the oven to 140°C fan-forced (160°C conventional).

For the terrine, carefully pick over the chicken to check for any bone or cartilage and remove half of the skin. Add all of the other ingredients to a large bowl along with the chicken and massage really well into the meat with your hands.

Lay the chicken in the terrine, alternating the skinless thighs for the skin-on ones and placing the prunes in random places – remembering that when you cut the terrine you want some prune, but not too much, in each slice. Press down to compact the layers and cover with baking paper and foil. Place the terrine in a roasting tin and pour in enough hot water to come halfway up the mould. Carefully transfer to the oven and bake for 50 minutes, or until the internal temperature reaches 70°C. Remove from the water bath and rest for 15 minutes.

Remove the paper and foil and cut a thick cardboard template the same size as the inside of the mould. Wrap the template in foil, place on top of the terrine and weigh down with cans or other weights distributed evenly across the template. Place in the fridge overnight.

To make the dressing, mix the egg yolk, mustard, vinegar and a pinch of salt in a small bowl. Mix in the oil and cream until combined. This dressing isn't an emulsification and will have a slightly broken consistency.

Unmould the terrine, cut into slices and serve with the dressing and the garnishes on the side.

SERVES 8–10

1.6 kg chicken thighs, boned, skin left on
3 garlic cloves, finely grated
finely grated zest of 1 lemon
14 pitted prunes, cut in half
2 tablespoons chopped thyme leaves
1 tablespoon ground allspice
20 grates of whole nutmeg
1 teaspoon freshly ground black pepper
2½ tablespoons salt flakes

MUSTARD CREAM DRESSING
1 egg yolk
1 tablespoon Dijon mustard
1 teaspoon sherry vinegar
salt flakes
100 ml extra virgin olive oil
2 tablespoons cream

GARNISHES
2 large granny smith apples, thinly sliced, skin on
2 celery hearts, stalks separated with fine leaves attached
French tarragon or dill fronds, to serve
watercress, fine leaves picked, to serve

TIP
The mustard cream dressing will keep for up to 5 days in the fridge. It is also delicious tossed through freshly cooked potatoes or beans, spooned over a grilled fish fillet, or served with roast chicken.

PICKLED BABY OCTOPUS WITH RED WINE, TOMATO & OREGANO

Slowly cooking octopus infuses it with all of the intense flavours of the braising liquor and ensures that it's perfectly tender. This is delicious warm from the pan, but even better the next day — just bring to room temperature first and serve with plenty of bread to mop up the juices.

Blanch the octopus in a large pot of boiling salted water for 3 minutes. Drain and set aside.

Heat the oil in a large, heavy-based saucepan over medium heat. Add the shallots, garlic and chillies and cook, stirring often, for about 5 minutes, or until the shallots are softened and starting to caramelise. Add the wine, oregano, thyme, bay leaves, coriander seeds, passata, tomato paste and 600 ml of water, season and bring to a simmer. Add the octopus, bring back to a simmer and cook over low heat for 30 minutes.

Add the cherry tomatoes and vinegar to the pan, stir through and cook for a further 20 minutes. As the tomatoes cook, pull the skins away from the flesh with tongs and discard. Stir through the sugar and adjust the seasoning if necessary. The liquid should have thickened to a sauce-like consistency.

Serve warm or cool to room temperature. If making ahead of time, place in a jar and keep in the fridge for up to a week.

SERVES 10

- 1 kg cleaned baby octopus
- 100 ml extra virgin olive oil
- 10 French shallots, peeled and thickly sliced
- 6 garlic cloves, peeled and smashed
- 3 small red chillies, split lengthways
- 400 ml red wine
- 2 tablespoons dried Greek-style oregano
- 3 thyme sprigs
- 2 fresh bay leaves
- 1 tablespoon coriander seeds
- 200 ml passata
- 2 tablespoons tomato paste
- salt flakes and freshly ground black pepper
- 250 g cherry tomatoes
- 4 tablespoons sherry vinegar
- 1 heaped tablespoon raw sugar

SPICED SPINACH, YOGHURT & PINE NUT DIP

Spinach dip can often be a pretty bland affair, but building depth of flavour with sautéed garlic and leek, cumin and a hint of smoky paprika makes all the difference.

Heat the oil in a wide-based saucepan over medium heat, add the garlic and fry until fragrant. Add the leek, cumin and paprika and cook, stirring, for 5 minutes. Add the spinach and cook for about 6 minutes, covered, stirring occasionally. Season and set aside to cool.

Drain a little liquid from the spinach, then puree with the yoghurt and half the pine nuts until you have a smooth paste. Spread onto your serving plate, squeeze over some lemon, scatter over the remaining pine nuts, dress with a little oil and serve with flatbread.

MAKES ABOUT 400 G

4 tablespoons extra virgin olive oil, plus extra
5 garlic cloves, finely sliced
1 leek, white and pale green parts, finely sliced
1 teaspoon ground cumin
½ teaspoon sweet smoked paprika
250 g baby spinach
salt flakes and freshly ground black pepper
150 g thick plain yoghurt
80 g pine nuts, toasted
½ lemon
flatbread, to serve

ROASTED BEETROOT, CINNAMON & POMEGRANATE DIP

Cinnamon is such a warm spice and works beautifully with roasted beetroot and the caramelised sweetness and sharp tang of pomegranate molasses.

Preheat the oven to 180°C fan-forced (200°C conventional).

Place the beetroot pieces in a baking dish, drizzle with oil, season with salt and pepper, add 2 teaspoons of cinnamon and the allspice and toss through to evenly coat. Add a splash of water to the dish, cover with baking paper and foil and roast for 40–60 minutes until tender. Remove the paper and foil and bake for another 15 minutes – the beetroot will be tender and starting to caramelise. Remove from the oven and set aside to cool.

Once cooled, puree the beetroot with the chilli powder until smooth. Add the yoghurt and pomegranate molasses and process until combined. Adjust the seasoning if necessary.

To serve, spread the beetroot dip onto a serving plate, crumble over the feta, sprinkle on a little extra cinnamon, scatter over the pomegranate seeds (if using) and mint and serve with flatbread.

MAKES ABOUT 800 G

900 g beetroot, scrubbed, trimmed and cut in sixths
extra virgin olive oil
salt flakes and freshly ground black pepper
2 teaspoons ground cinnamon, plus extra
1 teaspoon ground allspice
1 teaspoon chilli powder
300 g thick plain yoghurt
4 tablespoons pomegranate molasses
100 g feta
2 handfuls of pomegranate seeds (optional)
1 handful of mint leaves
flatbread, to serve

PITA BREAD

You can cook these in a frying pan, on a flat grill or even the bar grill of a barbecue for a slightly smoky charred flavour. They're great with dips, falafel, salads and grilled and slow-roasted meats. Try them with my meltingly tender Greek Lamb Shoulder (see page 170) for the best souvlaki you'll ever have.

1 sachet (7 g) dried yeast
10 g caster sugar
1 teaspoon salt
300 g plain unbleached flour, plus extra
50 g fine semolina, plus extra
½ tablespoon extra virgin olive oil

Dissolve the yeast and sugar in 65 ml of warm water and set aside for 15 minutes (the mix will froth and expand, so use a medium-sized container or jug).

Dissolve the salt in 125 ml of cold water.

Add the flour and semolina to a large bowl and mix. Make a well in the centre, add the yeast mixture, salt water and oil and work in the bowl until you form a dough. Tip onto a floured surface and knead for about 10 minutes. The dough should be smooth and elastic. Shape the dough into a ball and place in a large clean bowl, cover with a damp tea towel and set aside in a warm place to prove. The dough is ready when it has roughly doubled in volume. This will take 40 minutes, or longer, depending on the room temperature.

Punch down the risen dough, divide into egg-sized pieces and roll into balls. Once rolled, rest each ball under a damp tea towel while you portion the remaining dough. Line these up systematically so that you roll out the first ball you made and work your way to the last; this way they will rest for a similar length of time. Lightly flour your benchtop, scatter over a little semolina and roll out the balls into oblongs or circles about 5-mm thick.

Heat a dry frying pan or a barbecue grill over high heat. Cook the pitas for a couple of minutes on each side until they bubble and are lightly browned. Once cooked, place on a clean tea towel, stacked two high, then lay over another tea towel.

This recipe can be multiplied and any leftover cooked pita can be stored in a plastic bag in the fridge or frozen for later use.

MAKES 8–10 PITAS

FOCACCIA WITH RED ONION, ROSEMARY, OLIVES & CHILLI

This is perfect with a selection of antipasti, but also pretty delicious on its own.

Mix the flour, semolina and 1 teaspoon of salt in a large bowl.

Dissolve the yeast and sugar in a large jug with 320 ml of warm water and set aside for 3 minutes. The mix will start to foam.

Make a well in the flour mix, pour in the yeast solution and bring together into a dough. Tip onto a floured benchtop and knead for 5 minutes. The dough should be soft and silky. Place in a large clean bowl, cover with plastic wrap and set aside in a warm place to prove.

Sprinkle a 60 cm × 40 cm baking tray (or trays, you can shape the dough into loaves of any size) with a little semolina. Once the dough has doubled in size (about 45 minutes, but this will depend on how warm the room is) tip onto the prepared tray and press into place with your fingertips. Sprinkle with a little semolina, cover with a tea towel and prove again in a warm place for 20 minutes, or until it swells and puffs up.

Preheat the oven to 180°C fan-forced (200°C conventional).

Heat a little oil in a large frying pan and cook the onion and garlic until softened and coloured. Add 100 ml of water, season and cook until mostly dry. Toss with the rosemary and olives.

Once the focaccia has risen, indent the surface with your fingertips to hold the topping. Drop the onion mix on top, sprinkle with the dried chilli flakes, drizzle with a little oil, season with salt and pepper and bake for 20–30 minutes, or until golden. Cool on the tray before cutting.

MAKES 2 × 300 G LOAVES

400 g plain flour
100 g fine semolina, plus extra
salt flakes and freshly ground black pepper
1 sachet (7 g) dried yeast
2 pinches of caster sugar
extra virgin olive oil
2 red onions, peeled and sliced in thick wedges with the root still attached
4 garlic cloves, sliced
1 rosemary sprig, leaves stripped and chopped
2 handfuls of black olives, pitted and torn
2 teaspoons dried chilli flakes

POTATO CHIP TORTILLA WITH SRIRACHA MAYONNAISE

The idea for this comes from a Ferran Adrià take on Spain's classic tortilla de patatas. *I can't imagine it ever crossed the pass at elBulli, but it is quite delicious. Eat it warm with a cold beer.*

To make the sriracha mayonnaise, combine all the ingredients in a small bowl. Refrigerate with plastic wrap pressed against the surface of the mayonnaise to stop a skin forming.

To make the tortilla, whisk the eggs and cream in a large bowl until combined. Add the potato chips to the egg mix and gently stir through. Set aside for 10 minutes or so, mixing through every now and then.

Once the chips have softened, heat a medium, non-stick frying pan over medium heat. Heat the oil and pour in the tortilla mix. Stir the mix through quickly, then flatten out with a spatula and cook for 5 minutes, loosening the sides with your spatula as it sets.

Take off the heat and lay a plate over the tortilla. Turn the pan over while holding the plate and then carefully remove the pan. Slide the tortilla off the plate and back into the pan to cook the other side. Cook for a further couple of minutes, or until set, then turn out onto a plate again and set aside to cool for 5 minutes.

Spoon the sriracha mayo over the tortilla, garnish with coriander, drizzle on some extra sriracha chilli sauce and serve.

SERVES 8–10

10 eggs
100 ml cream
250 g good-quality salted potato chips
1 tablespoon extra virgin olive oil
1 handful of coriander leaves
sriracha chilli sauce, to serve

SRIRACHA MAYONNAISE
4 tablespoons mayonnaise
2 tablespoons sriracha chilli sauce
2 teaspoons Worcestershire sauce

CHICKEN, PRAWN & SHIITAKE POT-STICKER DUMPLINGS

I'm a real sucker for a good dumpling. So are my girls. I'd make them a lot more often if I had the time; at least once a week, possibly even twice. They freeze well, so making a big batch like this may take a little time, but you'll be glad you did.

To make the dipping sauce, add all of the ingredients to a small bowl and mix until combined and the sugar has dissolved.

To make the dumpling filling, combine the chicken mince and sliced prawns in a large bowl. Add the oyster sauce, sesame oil, soy sauce, chestnuts, ginger, spring onion and shiitake and combine well.

Lay three or four wonton wrappers on a dry benchtop, moisten the top edges with a little water and place 1 tablespoon of the filling in the centre of each. Bring the edges together and press in pleats to seal. Repeat until the filling is used up. Chill the dumplings on a tray in the fridge until ready to cook. Dumplings can also be frozen at this point. Freeze in layers with baking paper between each layer so that they don't stick together. Once frozen, they can be stacked or bagged.

Heat a tablespoon of oil in a deep-sided, flat-bottomed, non-stick frying pan over high heat. Add enough dumplings to snugly fit the pan (about 20 dumplings), pleated side up, and cook for 2–4 minutes until deep golden on the bottom. Add 250 ml of hot water and cover tightly so that no steam escapes. Cook for 5–6 minutes, or until all the water is absorbed and the dumplings are cooked (break one open to check). Serve immediately with the dipping sauce on the side. Repeat for the remaining dumplings if required, otherwise freeze.

MAKES ABOUT 45 DUMPLINGS

250 g chicken thigh mince
8 large green prawn cutlets, tail removed and flesh finely sliced
1 tablespoon oyster sauce
½ teaspoon sesame oil
1 tablespoon light soy sauce
1 × 150 g can water chestnuts, drained and chopped
6-cm piece of ginger, finely chopped
4 spring onions, finely sliced
6 shiitake mushrooms, finely sliced
1 × 275 g packet gow gee or wonton wrappers
vegetable oil

GINGER–SOY DIPPING SAUCE

120 ml light soy sauce
1 teaspoon sesame oil
2 teaspoons caster sugar
1 small red chilli, finely sliced
6-cm piece of ginger, finely julienned

TIP
Leftover ginger–soy dipping sauce can be spooned over rice or steamed fish, used to lightly stir-fry some vegetables, or served alongside any kind of dumplings or spring rolls.

ROAST DUCK, MUSHROOM & CORIANDER RICE PAPER ROLLS

Roast duck transforms the humble rice paper roll into deluxe little treats. It's a bit of a commitment to get these prepped, but once you get the hang of rolling, they'll come together quickly. Well worth the effort.

Cook the noodles according to the packet instructions, drain, refresh in cold water and drain again. Cut into 15-cm lengths.

Dissolve the sugar in the fish sauce and dress the mushrooms. Set aside for 5 minutes, mixing occasionally.

Set your ingredients up on a clean bench in a row so that you are able to work systematically – coriander, duck, fried shallots, chilli, mushrooms, bean sprouts, iceberg and vermicelli – leaving enough space to roll in front of you.

Fill a large shallow bowl with hot water and, working with one at a time, immerse a rice paper round in the water (do this reasonably quickly as they will soften further on the bench, but if they are too soft they become hard to work with), lay the round on the clean bench and start adding your ingredients one at a time to form a line just below the centre of the round. Fold the edge closest to you over the filling and roll over, folding the sides in tightly as you do. The roll will seal itself once fully rolled. Set aside and repeat. Don't refrigerate unless you absolutely have to.

For the dipping sauce, mix the coconut cream and hoisin together, sprinkle over some fried shallots and coriander and serve with the rolls.

MAKES ABOUT 26 ROLLS

100 g rice vermicelli
½ teaspoon caster sugar
1 tablespoon fish sauce
1 punnet small Swiss brown mushrooms, finely sliced
½ bunch of coriander, leaves picked and chopped
2 Chinese-style roast duck breasts, finely sliced
3 tablespoons fried shallots, lightly ground
2 long green chillies, finely sliced
2 large handfuls of bean sprouts, blanched in boiling water for 5 seconds and refreshed in cold water
¼ iceberg lettuce, finely shredded
1 packet medium Vietnamese rice paper rounds

COCONUT–HOISIN DIPPING SAUCE

150 ml quality coconut cream
3 heaped tablespoons hoisin sauce
fried shallots, to garnish
chopped coriander leaves, to garnish

PRAWN BAGUETTE WITH MINTED CABBAGE & SUMAC

These are perhaps a little indulgent, but they're a perfect way to use up any leftover prawns on Boxing Day, and a hamper of these at the beach will make the family forever grateful (I wish!). Don't skimp on the quality of the bread and be generous with the butter.

Grill the pancetta under a hot grill until crisp.

In a large bowl, toss the cabbage with the mint. Dress with oil, season, squeeze over lemon juice to taste and toss to coat. Set aside for 5 minutes for the cabbage to soften.

Toss the prawns with a little oil and 1 tablespoon of sumac.

Split the baguettes down the middle and butter generously. Add sriracha chilli sauce to taste and fill with the dressed cabbage and prawns. Top with the pancetta, squeeze over some lemon juice, sprinkle with extra sumac and serve.

SERVES 6

12 slices of pancetta
¼ large white cabbage, shredded
2 handfuls of mint leaves, shredded
extra virgin olive oil
salt flakes and freshly ground black pepper
1 lemon
24 small cooked prawns, peeled and deveined
1 tablespoon sumac, plus extra
6 long baguette-style rolls
butter, at room temperature
sriracha chilli sauce, to taste

FILO PIE WITH GREENS, RICOTTA & PUMPKIN SEEDS

This is one of my many versions of spanakopita. I can't help fiddling with dishes that I cook all the time, plus I'm lucky enough to get surprise deliveries of armloads of rocket, chard, herbs and leeks, amongst other things, from Mike's folks' garden. They all make it in, at one time or another.

Preheat the oven to 180°C fan-forced (200°C conventional).

In a large saucepan over medium heat, add a small knob of butter and cook the onion and garlic for 5 minutes, or until softened. Add the silverbeet, cover and cook for 15 minutes over low heat, stirring occasionally. Add the spinach and parsley to the pan and stir through. Cook for a further 5 minutes, or until the spinach has wilted, then season. Tip into a sieve and drain all the excess liquid from the greens by pressing lightly. Cool for 5 minutes and then chop roughly.

Add the eggs, ricotta, crumbled feta, dill and nutmeg to a large bowl, season with salt and pepper and mix together. Add the chopped greens and mix until combined.

Melt the remaining butter and brush a baking dish with a little of it. Brush the sheets of filo one by one as you lay them into the buttered baking dish, carefully pushing the pastry into the corners and leaving enough overhanging to form a lid. You should need 20–25 sheets, depending on the shape and size of your dish.

Tip the filling into the dish and flatten out evenly. Fold the overhanging layers in, brushing the sheets with butter as you go. If you have a gap in the centre of the pie lid, fill it with some extra buttered and folded sheets. Brush the top of the pie with butter, scatter over the pumpkin seeds and bake for 25–30 minutes until golden.

SERVES 6–8

150 g butter
½ brown onion, finely diced
5 garlic cloves, finely chopped
1 bunch of silverbeet, sliced across in 2-cm widths including most of the stem
400 g English spinach
½ bunch of flat-leaf parsley, roughly chopped
salt flakes and freshly ground black pepper
4 eggs
375 g fresh ricotta
150 g feta
½ bunch of dill, fronds picked and finely chopped
3 big pinches of freshly grated nutmeg
1 × 375 g packet filo pastry, preferably chilled, not frozen
1 handful of pumpkin seeds

SOUP

GAZPACHO RODRIGUEZ 58
SPINACH, PEA & POTATO SOUP 60
AVGOLEMONO 63
SPICED TOMATO & CHILLI SOUP WITH SMOKED BACON 64
ROAST PUMPKIN SOUP WITH THAI FLAVOURS & YOUNG COCONUT 66
SPICED LENTIL & POTATO SOUP 69
PASTA E FAGIOLI 70

GAZPACHO RODRIGUEZ

My good friend (and gifted cook) Emma kindly shared this recipe with me. She spent ten years cooking professionally in Spain and this was a summer staple in her restaurant. It's based on an old family recipe, with a few tweaks here and there. The garnish of chopped or sliced vegetables is a traditional way to enhance the flavours of the soup and add texture.

Preheat the oven to 150°C fan-forced (170°C conventional).

Cut the tomatoes, capsicums, cucumbers and onion into roughly 3-cm chunks and add to a large bowl. Add the chopped parsley stalks to the bowl with 2 teaspoons of salt, mix through and set aside for 1 hour.

Cut the bread into thick slices, remove and discard any hard crusts, and place on a baking tray. Put the tray in the oven for 30 minutes, turning the slices over every now and then. The aim is to dry the bread out without actually toasting it. When the bread is crunchy, remove from the oven and turn the temperature up to 180°C fan-forced (200°C conventional).

Rub the bread all over with the garlic cloves and place in a large bowl, setting one slice aside for garnish.

Mix the sherry vinegar, half of the oil and 150 ml of water in a small bowl and pour over the bread. Set aside for 5–10 minutes until the bread has softened.

Rip up the reserved garlic bread and coat well in extra oil. Return to the oven and toast until you have golden croutons.

Add the soaked bread and the tomato mix to the bowl of a food processor and blitz. Pour in the remaining oil while processing.

Pass the soup through a sieve and adjust the salt, pepper and vinegar to taste.

Serve the gazpacho with the croutons, a splash of sherry vinegar and a drizzle of oil. Serve the tomatoes, cucumber, onion, capsicum, parsley and extra croutons on the side to add to the gazpacho as desired.

SERVES 6–8

2 kg ripe tomatoes
2 red capsicums, cored and deseeded
4 Lebanese cucumbers
1 white onion
3 large stalks of flat-leaf parsley, leaves picked, stalks chopped
salt flakes and freshly ground black pepper
1 loaf of quality ciabatta or white sourdough
3 small garlic cloves, germ removed
3 tablespoons sherry vinegar, plus extra
150 ml extra virgin olive oil (nothing too peppery or intense), plus extra

GARNISH
small heirloom tomatoes, sliced or whole if very small
Lebanese cucumber, finely sliced
white onion, finely sliced
red capsicum, finely sliced
parsley leaves

SPINACH, PEA & POTATO SOUP

This is such a rich and velvety soup. The luscious texture comes from slowly cooking the potatoes in butter. They add an earthy warmth and silky richness that works so well with the blitzed greens and peppery horseradish.

Melt the butter with a splash of oil in a large, wide-based saucepan over medium heat. Add the garlic, onion, leek, bay leaf and fennel seeds, stir and cook for 10 minutes. Add the potato, season and cook for a further 10 minutes, or until the potato is soft and breaking up. Add the stock and bring up to a simmer. Add the peas and cook for 5 minutes. Add the parsley and spinach and cook for 5 more minutes.

Take the soup off the heat and blitz with a hand-held blender until smooth. Adjust the seasoning if necessary. Serve the soup with freshly grated horseradish and a dollop of goat's curd.

SERVES 6–8

80 g butter
extra virgin olive oil
4 garlic cloves, finely chopped
1 small brown onion, finely diced
2 leeks, white and pale green parts, finely sliced
1 fresh bay leaf
2 teaspoons fennel seeds
3 large waxy potatoes, peeled and very finely sliced
salt flakes and freshly ground black pepper
1 litre chicken stock
200 g frozen peas
½ bunch of flat-leaf parsley, leaves picked and chopped
400 g English spinach
fresh horseradish (or unsweetened prepared horseradish), grated, to serve
goat's curd, to serve

AVGOLEMONO

This is my version of the classic Greek chicken and lemon soup. The 'double stock' makes a deep golden broth that is so delicious and nourishing. Serve as soon as the egg sets in the hot broth, and eat with fresh crusty bread.

Preheat the oven to 200°C fan-forced (220°C conventional).

Toss the chicken wings in a little oil and season with salt and pepper. Place on a baking tray and roast for 30 minutes, or until golden.

Place the chicken wings in a stockpot, cover with the stock and 1 litre of water. Add the bay leaves, thyme and smashed garlic. Bring to the boil and then simmer for 30 minutes, or until the chicken is very tender. Strain, reserving the stock.

When the chicken is cool enough to handle, pick all the meat from the bones and chop – I like to shred and use some of the skin too, but it's definitely optional.

Heat a good splash of oil in a large, wide-based saucepan over medium heat. Add the onion, chopped garlic and celery and cook, stirring frequently, for 10 minutes. Add the reserved stock and bring to a simmer. Add the pasta and cook until just al dente. Add the chicken meat and skin (if using) to the pan and quickly bring back to a simmer. Adjust the seasoning if necessary.

Crack the eggs into a small bowl and whisk in the lemon juice with a little salt and pepper. Pour the egg mix into the simmering soup, stir through for 1 minute and turn off the heat. Stir through the parsley and serve.

SERVES 4–6

- 1 kg chicken wings
- extra virgin olive oil
- salt flakes and freshly ground black pepper
- 2 litres chicken stock
- 2 fresh bay leaves
- 4 thyme sprigs
- 8 garlic cloves, 4 smashed, skin on, 4 peeled and chopped
- 1 large brown onion, finely diced
- 3 celery stalks, finely sliced
- 200 g pastina or risoni
- 4 eggs
- juice of 1 lemon
- 1 handful of flat-leaf parsley leaves, chopped

SPICED TOMATO & CHILLI SOUP WITH SMOKED BACON

This spicy soup can mostly be conjured from staples with a little help from the herb garden. Serve with plenty of generously buttered toast.

Preheat the oven to 180°C fan-forced (200°C conventional).

Add the drained tomatoes, chilli, onion, garlic, thyme, paprika, fennel seeds, cumin and olive oil to a large roasting tin, season with salt and pepper, toss through and bake for 50 minutes.

Add the roasted tomato mix, reserved tomato juice, chicken stock and tomato paste to a large saucepan and simmer over medium heat for 25 minutes. Blitz the soup with a hand-held blender. Add the cream and mix through, bring up to the boil and turn off the heat. Adjust the seasoning if necessary.

Fry the bacon in a non-stick frying pan over medium heat until brown and crisp. Toss the bacon with the chopped parsley.

Serve the soup with a dollop of sour cream, a sprinkling of bacon and slices of buttered toast.

SERVES 8–10

2 × 400 g cans whole tomatoes, drained and juice reserved
2 long red chillies, chopped
1 red onion, sliced in thick rounds
4 garlic cloves, sliced
3 thyme sprigs, leaves picked
1 teaspoon sweet smoked paprika
1 teaspoon fennel seeds
2 teaspoons ground cumin
100 ml extra virgin olive oil
salt flakes and freshly ground black pepper
1 litre chicken stock
2 tablespoons tomato paste
150 ml cream
6 rashers smoked bacon, finely chopped
1 handful of flat-leaf parsley leaves, chopped
sour cream, to serve
sliced sourdough bread, toasted, to serve
butter, to serve

ROAST PUMPKIN SOUP WITH THAI FLAVOURS & YOUNG COCONUT

The sweetness of the pumpkin, especially once roasted, balances so well with the hot and punchy flavours of Thai cuisine. Using prepared tom yum paste is a tasty shortcut, but pick a Thai brand – they usually have the best balance and flavour intensity.

Preheat the oven to 160°C fan-forced (180°C conventional).

Rub the pumpkin and onion with olive oil, season and roast for 1 hour, or until cooked. Once cool enough to handle, scoop out the pumpkin flesh and set aside.

Add the coconut oil to a large, wide-based saucepan over medium heat. Add the roasted onion, garlic and chilli, stir and cook for 3 minutes. Add the tom yum paste and cook for a further minute. Add the pumpkin flesh, fish sauce, coconut water, sugar and 500 ml of water, bring up to a simmer and cook for 20 minutes.

Take the soup off the heat, add the lime juice and puree with a hand-held blender until smooth. Adjust the seasoning to taste with a little more fish sauce or salt. Serve the soup topped with some coconut flesh, coriander leaves, a drizzle of coconut cream and a sprinkling of fried shallots.

SERVES 10

½ large Kent pumpkin (2.5 kg), cut in half and deseeded
3 red onions, peeled and cut in large chunks
extra virgin olive oil
salt flakes and freshly ground black pepper
40 ml virgin coconut oil (if in a solid state use 1 heaped tablespoon)
4 garlic cloves, finely sliced
3 small red chillies, finely sliced
3 tablespoons good-quality tom yum paste
2 tablespoons fish sauce, plus extra
1 litre coconut water
1½ tablespoons grated palm sugar
juice of 1 lime
1 young coconut, flesh removed
coriander leaves, to serve
coconut cream, to serve
fried shallots, to serve

SPICED LENTIL & POTATO SOUP

A Northern Greek peasant soup that Mike's mother makes inspired this recipe. She eats hers with torn bread and a hunk of feta. I like this earthier, spicier version with coriander and a good dollop of thick yoghurt.

Heat the oil in a large, heavy-based saucepan. Add the onion, leek, garlic, celery, chilli, cinnamon, pepper and cumin and cook over medium heat, stirring frequently, for 10 minutes. Add the potato, stir and cook for another 3 minutes. Add the tomatoes, lentils, crumbled stock cubes and 3 litres of water and bring to a simmer. Reduce the heat and simmer very slowly for 1 hour. As the soup cooks you may need to add a little more water to keep it from sticking.

Adjust the seasoning and serve with a dollop of yoghurt, a squeeze of lemon, a sprinkling of coriander leaves and some warmed mountain bread on the side.

SERVES 6–8

100 ml extra virgin olive oil
1 brown onion, diced
3 leeks, white and pale green parts, sliced in rounds
6 garlic cloves, sliced
4 celery stalks, finely sliced
2 small red chillies, chopped
1 teaspoon ground cinnamon
1 teaspoon freshly ground black pepper
2 teaspoons ground cumin
2 potatoes, peeled and cut in 1-cm dice
1 × 400 g can diced tomatoes
250 g brown lentils, washed
2 vegetable stock cubes
salt flakes and freshly ground black pepper
Greek-style yoghurt, to serve
lemon, to serve
coriander leaves, to serve
mountain bread, to serve

PASTA E FAGIOLI

This classic Italian soup really is a meal in itself. Choose a good extra virgin olive oil to dress this with, something piquant and peppery.

Melt the butter with 2½ tablespoons of oil in a large, wide-based saucepan over medium–low heat. Add the onion, garlic, carrot and celery, season, stir and cook until softened and sticky but not quite caramelised, about 10–15 minutes. Add the rosemary, bay leaves and tomato paste and fry briefly. Add the fennel, zucchini and green beans, turn up the heat and cook, stirring frequently, for 10 minutes. Add the stock, cannellini beans and 800 ml of water, stir, bring up to the boil and simmer for 10 minutes. Add the peas, pasta and parsley and cook for 5–10 minutes, or until the pasta is just cooked. Turn off the heat and adjust the seasoning to taste.

To serve, top each bowl of soup with some grated Grana Padano and a good drizzle of extra virgin olive oil.

SERVES 6

50 g butter
extra virgin olive oil
2 brown onions, finely diced
4 garlic cloves, finely sliced
2 carrots, finely sliced
4 celery stalks, finely sliced
salt flakes and freshly ground black pepper
2 rosemary sprigs, leaves stripped and chopped
2 fresh bay leaves
2 tablespoons tomato paste
1 small fennel bulb, finely diced
2 zucchini, sliced in half moons
200 g green beans, cut into short lengths
1 litre chicken stock
1 × 400 g can cannellini beans, drained and rinsed well
120 g frozen peas
250 g small macaroni
½ bunch of flat-leaf parsley, leaves picked and chopped
Grana Padano cheese, finely grated, to serve

SALADS *and* VEGETABLES

- MIXED LEAF & HERB SALAD WITH SIMPLE FRENCH VINAIGRETTE 74
- VINAIGRETTE POTATO SALAD WITH SHREDDED CABBAGE, CARAWAY & LEMON 76
- CELERIAC, APPLE & KALE SLAW WITH SMOKED ALMONDS & DEHYDRATED ANCHOVIES 79
- EGG & BACON SALAD WITH CURLY ENDIVE, JERUSALEM ARTICHOKE, SHALLOTS & CORNICHONS 80
- BEETROOT, QUINOA & SPINACH SALAD WITH HALOUMI, SULTANAS & DILL 82
- FENNEL, ORANGE, CURRANT & OLIVE SALAD 85
- BUTTER LETTUCE, TOMATO, AVOCADO, MOZZARELLA & PICKLED JALAPEÑO SALAD 86
- MY GO-TO TUNA SALAD 88
- TUNA SALAD WITH CUCUMBER, TOMATO, BEETROOT, RADISH & OLIVES 91
- COLD SOBA NOODLES WITH AVOCADO, BEAN SPROUTS, SOY, GINGER & SESAME 92
- CHICKEN VERMICELLI SALAD WITH YOUNG COCONUT, ASIAN HERBS & NUOC CHAM 94
- BROAD BEANS & PEAS WITH JAMON & MINT 97
- ROASTED CAULIFLOWER & PARSNIP WITH CUMIN, CHILLI & PARMESAN 98
- GRILLED EGGPLANT WITH TAHINI & YOGHURT DRESSING, POMEGRANATE, CHILLI & MINT 100
- BROCCOLINI WITH BACON, SHALLOTS, GARLIC & CHILLI 103
- ROASTED CARROTS WITH RAISINS, HARISSA & CORIANDER 104
- SPICED PUMPKIN & SWEET POTATO BAKE WITH PICKLED ONION & HALOUMI 106
- RATATOUILLE 109

MIXED LEAF & HERB SALAD WITH SIMPLE FRENCH VINAIGRETTE

It could be snowing outside and I'd still have a mixed leaf salad on the table. In summer I love the freshness of crisply cold leaves, in winter I love the refreshing contrast with rich and hearty dishes.

For the vinaigrette, mash the garlic, salt and mustard together in a small bowl until you have an even paste. Add the lemon juice and vinegar and combine. Add the oil and plenty of black pepper and beat with a fork until emulsified.

Combine the salad leaves, celery leaves and stalks, and herbs in a large bowl. Beat the dressing again to re-emulsify and pour over the salad – you won't need all the dressing, just enough to coat the leaves. Toss the salad carefully using forked fingers so as not to bruise the leaves.

Pile into a large serving bowl and serve immediately. Leftover dressing will keep well in the fridge.

SERVES 4–6

TIP

This classic French vinaigrette is so versatile – toss it through any leafy green salad, or add it to freshly cooked chickpeas and crumble some feta over the top for a lovely side dish. It's also delicious with my Chicken, Olive, Lentil and Radicchio Salad (see page 154). The vinaigrette will keep in the fridge for up to 5 days.

1 iceberg lettuce, leaves torn
1 small radicchio, leaves torn
2 witlof, leaves separated
1 celery heart, pale yellow leaves picked and stalks finely sliced on an angle
5 flat-leaf parsley stalks, leaves picked and torn
½ bunch of chives, snipped into 2-cm pieces
½ bunch of chervil, picked

FRENCH VINAIGRETTE

1 large garlic clove, finely grated
1 tablespoon salt flakes
1 tablespoon Dijon mustard
juice of ½ lemon
1½ tablespoons white wine vinegar
150 ml extra virgin olive oil
freshly ground black pepper

VINAIGRETTE POTATO SALAD WITH SHREDDED CABBAGE, CARAWAY & LEMON

When I was an apprentice my head chef once made a dish of potatoes in vinaigrette for lunch, and though it doesn't sound like much it was a bit of a revelation at the time. Potato salad was always such a stodgy affair, while this was just so fresh and vibrant. I've loved them in countless variations ever since.

Cook the potato in boiling salted water with the caraway seeds until tender. Drain well.

Combine the lemon juice, vinegar, oil and garlic in a large bowl. Add the hot potatoes and toss through. Adjust the seasoning if necessary and set aside for 5 minutes.

Add the cabbage to another large bowl, season with salt and pepper and toss. Set aside for 5 minutes to soften.

Add the softened cabbage to the potato and combine. Pile into a large bowl and serve.

SERVES 6–8

4 large Dutch cream potatoes, peeled and cut in sixths
2 teaspoons caraway seeds
juice of 1 large lemon
4 tablespoons white wine vinegar
4 tablespoons extra virgin olive oil
1 large garlic clove, finely grated
salt flakes and freshly ground black pepper
¼ large white cabbage, finely shredded

CELERIAC, APPLE & KALE SLAW WITH SMOKED ALMONDS & DEHYDRATED ANCHOVIES

This healthful salad is delicious on its own, or with pork, roast chicken or full-flavoured fish. Be sure to shred the kale very finely and don't worry if it seems like a lot of dressing, you'll need it to soften the kale.

Preheat the oven to 180°C fan-forced (200°C conventional).

Drizzle the whole garlic bulb with olive oil, wrap in foil and roast for 30–35 minutes until fragrant and soft. Unwrap and set aside until cool enough to handle.

While the garlic roasts, lay the anchovies out flat on a lined baking tray and place in the oven for 5 minutes, or until they're brown with a powdery appearance. Set aside to cool and dehydrate further.

Squeeze the garlic paste into a small bowl (you should have about 2 heaped tablespoons), mash up with a fork and mix in the sour cream, lemon juice, 4 tablespoons of oil and a splash of water. Season with salt and pepper.

Combine the celeriac, kale, apple and mint in a large bowl. Add the dressing and toss well. Tip the slaw into your serving bowl, crumble over the dried anchovies, scatter over the almonds and serve.

SERVES 6

- 1 large garlic bulb
- 4 tablespoons extra virgin olive oil, plus extra
- 10 high-quality anchovy fillets (pink and fleshy ones)
- 150 g sour cream
- juice of 1 lemon
- salt flakes and freshly ground black pepper
- 1 small celeriac, peeled and julienned
- 1 bunch of kale, leaves stripped and finely shredded
- 2 granny smith apples, thinly sliced and slices cut in half
- 2 handfuls of mint leaves, finely chopped
- 2 handfuls of smoked almonds, roughly chopped

EGG & BACON SALAD WITH CURLY ENDIVE, JERUSALEM ARTICHOKE, SHALLOTS & CORNICHONS

This is my version of the classic French salad of endive, egg and hot bacon dressing.

Preheat the oven to 180°C fan-forced (200°C conventional). Line a baking tray with baking paper.

Oil and season the Jerusalem artichokes and roast on the prepared tray for 30 minutes, or until tender. Set aside.

Cook the shallots in a saucepan of boiling salted water for 15 minutes until tender. Drain and peel. Pull apart the individual layers and set aside.

Place two large, non-stick frying pans over medium heat.

Fry the bacon in one of the pans until crisp, adding a little oil if necessary. When the bacon is almost ready, add the garlic and fry until fragrant. Take off the heat.

Fry the eggs sunny side up in a little oil in the other pan.

Add the shallots and vinegar to the bacon and toss through, adding a little more oil if dry.

Place some torn endive leaves on each of your plates, add the artichoke slices, cornichons and eggs, spoon over the bacon and shallot dressing, sprinkle over some chives and serve with rye toast.

SERVES 4

4 Jerusalem artichokes, scrubbed and cut into 2-cm thick slices
extra virgin olive oil
salt flakes and freshly ground black pepper
6 French shallots, cut in half, skin on
350 g bacon, cut into lardons
2 garlic cloves, sliced
4 eggs, at room temperature
2½ tablespoons sherry vinegar
1 large densely packed head of curly endive, trimmed, coarse leaves discarded
10 cornichons, cut in half lengthways
½ bunch of chives, snipped
toasted rye bread, to serve

BEETROOT, QUINOA & SPINACH SALAD WITH HALOUMI, SULTANAS & DILL

I love the sweet, salty and vinegary accents in this earthy salad. It's perfect as part of a feast or packaged up for a healthy lunch on the go.

Preheat the oven to 200°C fan-forced (220°C conventional).

Place the beetroot on a double layer of foil. Drizzle over some oil, season with salt and pepper, wrap up and roast on a baking tray for 1–1½ hours until the beetroot is cooked.

In the meantime, add the quinoa to a saucepan of boiling water and simmer for 10 minutes until cooked. Drain.

Add the sultanas and 3 tablespoons of vinegar to a small saucepan, bring to the boil and take straight off the heat. Set aside.

Unwrap the cooked beetroot, cool a little and slip off the skins. Add the flesh to the bowl of a food processor and blitz to a rough puree. Tip the puree into a sieve and set aside to drain for 5 minutes (there's quite a lot of liquid in the beetroot and the salad will be too wet if you don't drain it).

Add the lemon juice, garlic, cumin, 100 ml of oil and the remaining vinegar to a large bowl, season with salt and pepper and combine. Add the drained quinoa to the dressing and mix. Add the beetroot, combine and set aside for 5 minutes.

Place the shredded spinach on your serving platter and top with the beetroot mix.

Pan-fry the slices of haloumi in a little oil in a large frying pan until golden brown. Drain briefly.

Arrange the haloumi on top of the salad, scatter over the sultanas, dill and sunflower seeds and serve.

SERVES 4–6

- 2 large beetroot, trimmed and quartered
- 100 ml extra virgin olive oil, plus extra
- salt flakes and freshly ground black pepper
- 300 g white quinoa, washed
- 3 tablespoons sultanas
- 120 ml red wine vinegar
- juice of 1 lemon
- 1 large garlic clove, finely grated
- 2 teaspoons ground cumin
- 3 handfuls of baby spinach, finely shredded
- 1 × 250 g packet of haloumi, cut into 8 slices
- 2 handfuls of dill fronds
- 3 tablespoons sunflower seeds

FENNEL, ORANGE, CURRANT & OLIVE SALAD

Make this during winter when fennel bulbs are fat and sweet, and navel oranges are at their best. I particularly love the sweet and salty combination of the currants and olives.

Add the vinegar, currants and chilli flakes to a small saucepan and simmer for 1 minute. Take off the heat, add the onion, oil and olives, mix through and set aside.

Pick and reserve the fine green fennel fronds and slice the bulb into wedges about 1-cm thick. Peel and slice the oranges.

Add the fennel wedges, orange and mint to a large bowl, season with salt and pepper and toss. Tip into your serving bowl, dress with the currant and olive mix, garnish with the fennel fronds and serve.

SERVES 4

4 tablespoons red wine vinegar
80 g currants
½ teaspoon dried chilli flakes
½ large red onion, finely diced
4 tablespoons extra virgin olive oil
80 g kalamata olives (or your favourite type), pitted
1 large fennel bulb
3 navel oranges
4 mint sprigs, leaves picked
salt flakes and freshly ground black pepper

BUTTER LETTUCE, TOMATO, AVOCADO, MOZZARELLA & PICKLED JALAPEÑO SALAD

This salad has a bit of the American steakhouse about it. It would be perfect with a big chargrilled rib eye dressed with a slick of virgin oil, a squeeze of lemon and a mound of fresh horseradish on the side.

Score a cross in the base of the tomato, plunge into boiling water for 1 minute and refresh in cold water. Peel off the skin and dice the flesh.

Mix the parsley and chilli together with a splash of oil.

Add the tomato, avocado, garlic, lemon juice and a good dash of oil to a bowl, season with salt and pepper and toss gently.

Arrange the butter lettuce and mozzarella on a serving platter, tip over the avocado and tomato mix, spoon over the chilli and parsley, scatter over the onion, drizzle with oil and serve.

SERVES 6

1 large ripe oxheart tomato
2 handfuls of flat-leaf parsley leaves, finely chopped
2 pickled jalapeños, finely chopped
extra virgin olive oil
1 ripe avocado, diced
1 small garlic clove, finely grated
juice of 1 lemon
salt flakes and freshly ground black pepper
2 large heads of butter lettuce, trimmed, heart quartered and large leaves left whole
2 large balls of fior di latte mozzarella, torn
10 cocktail onions, sliced in rounds

MY GO-TO TUNA SALAD

No tricks here, just chop, season and mix. It's my go-to salad when I'm on the run.

Add the tuna, tomato, parsley, pickle, avocado, cucumber and sunflower seeds to a large bowl, season with salt and pepper and dress with oil. Add the vinegar and Tabasco to taste, toss gently and serve.

SERVES 2

1 × 185 g can tuna in spring water, drained
1 large ripe tomato, cut into small wedges
2 handfuls of flat-leaf parsley leaves
2 dill pickles, finely chopped
1 avocado, diced
1 Lebanese cucumber, peeled, deseeded and chopped
1 handful of sunflower seeds (or pumpkin seeds)
salt flakes and freshly ground black pepper
extra virgin olive oil
vinegar (or lemon juice), to taste
Tabasco sauce, to taste

TUNA SALAD WITH CUCUMBER, TOMATO, BEETROOT, RADISH & OLIVES

This is almost more of an antipasto selection than a salad. The charm lies in the selection of sparkling fresh vegetables and the best tuna in olive oil that you can find.

Preheat the oven to 180°C fan-forced (200°C conventional).

Cut the pita into eight triangles, open each piece out and bake in the oven for a few minutes until crisping up.

Add a splash of oil and the butter beans to a large frying pan over high heat. Fry, tossing frequently, for 5–8 minutes until the bean skins are golden and crisp. Add the paprika, season, toss through quickly and tip into a bowl.

For the dressing, add the oil, lemon juice and vinegar to a small bowl, season with salt and pepper and stir to combine.

To assemble, spread the mayonnaise over the bottom of a large platter. Add the ingredients one by one: cucumber, onion, tuna, beans, tomatoes, radishes and beetroot. Scatter the olives over the salad and spoon over the dressing.

Serve immediately with the pita on the side.

SERVES 4

1 large round of pita bread
extra virgin olive oil
1 × 400 g can butter beans, drained and rinsed
1 teaspoon smoked paprika
salt flakes and freshly ground black pepper
3 heaped tablespoons mayonnaise
3 Lebanese cucumbers, peeled, deseeded and sliced
½ red onion, sliced in thin half moons
400 g tuna in oil, drained
250 g grape or cherry tomatoes, large ones cut in half
6 small red radishes, whole with a little of the leaf left on
4 baby beetroot or 1 small beetroot, very finely sliced
12 large kalamata olives

DRESSING
4 tablespoons extra virgin olive oil
juice of ½ lemon
1 tablespoon red wine vinegar
salt flakes and freshly ground black pepper

COLD SOBA NOODLES WITH AVOCADO, BEAN SPROUTS, SOY, GINGER & SESAME

I could easily eat good soba noodles with a little seasoning and dressing and not much else, but add some bean sprouts and avocado and you've got a deliciously light and healthy lunch. You could also add some shredded cooked chicken if you like.

Blanch the bean sprouts in boiling water for 5 seconds and refresh in cold water. Drain and gently squeeze out any moisture.

For the dressing, add the garlic, ginger, sugar, soy, lemon juice and sesame and olive oils to a large bowl and combine. Add the noodles and bean sprouts and mix well.

Pile the noodles into a serving bowl and top with the avocado, spring onion and pickled ginger. Shake over some nori and sesame seasoning and nanami togarashi.

Toss the noodles at the table and serve with more nanami togarashi and nori and sesame seasoning on the side.

SERVES 4

250 g bean sprouts
1 small garlic clove, finely grated
6-cm piece of ginger, finely grated
2 pinches of sugar
4 tablespoons light Japanese-style soy sauce
juice of 1 large lemon
1 teaspoon sesame oil
4 tablespoons extra virgin olive oil
1 × 270 g packet of soba noodles, cooked as per packet instructions, refreshed in iced water and drained
2 avocados, diced
4 spring onions, finely sliced
2 tablespoons pickled ginger
toasted nori and sesame seasoning (available from Asian grocers), to serve
nanami togarashi (Japanese chilli powder, available from Asian grocers), to serve

CHICKEN VERMICELLI SALAD WITH YOUNG COCONUT, ASIAN HERBS & NUOC CHAM

This Vietnamese-style salad makes a delicious lunch or light dinner, especially on a hot day.

Add the coconut water and enough water to just cover the chicken to a small saucepan. Add a splash of fish sauce, bring to a simmer and add the chicken breast. Poach for 8–12 minutes, turn off the heat and stand for 2 minutes in the water. The chicken will finish cooking in the hot water, but cooking time will vary a little depending on the size of the breast. Remove the chicken from the liquid and rest before slicing thinly.

Cook the noodles as per the packet instructions. Refresh in cold water, drain and cut into short lengths.

Blanch the bean sprouts for 5 seconds in boiling water. Drain and gently squeeze out any moisture.

For the nuoc cham, add the sugar, garlic, fish sauce and 2½ tablespoons of water to a small bowl and stir to dissolve the sugar. Mix in the remaining ingredients and set aside for 5 minutes before using. You can adjust the nuoc cham with more lime, sugar, chilli or fish sauce if necessary.

In a large bowl, combine the noodles with a splash of oil, the coconut flesh and lime juice. Add the mint, basil and coriander, reserving some herbs to garnish, and toss to combine.

Pile the noodle mix onto a serving plate, add the bean sprouts, sliced chicken, toasted coconut and remaining herbs and generously spoon over the nuoc cham. Serve immediately.

SERVES 2 GENEROUSLY OR 4 AS A SNACK

1 whole young coconut (drinking coconut), flesh chopped and water reserved
splash of fish sauce
1 large chicken breast
200 g bean thread noodles
3 handfuls of bean sprouts
rice bran or vegetable oil
juice of 1 lime
1 handful of Vietnamese mint leaves
1 handful of Thai basil leaves
1 handful of coriander leaves
1 handful of shaved coconut, toasted

NUOC CHAM

1½ tablespoons finely grated palm sugar
1 small garlic clove, smashed
3 tablespoons fish sauce
juice of 2 limes
2 tablespoons rice wine vinegar
1 lemongrass stem, white part only, finely chopped
2 small red chillies, finely chopped

TIP

Nuoc cham is the basis of so many Vietnamese dishes. Use it to dress any Asian-style salad, or spoon over steamed or roasted fish. It's also fabulous as a dipping sauce for spring rolls and fried or steamed dumplings. It will keep in the fridge for up to 4 days.

BROAD BEANS & PEAS WITH JAMON & MINT

Make this when broad beans are at their best. It's a bit of a labour of love, what with all the podding and podding again, but is well worth it. You could also simply make this with frozen peas for a quick version any time of year.

Cook the broad beans in boiling salted water for 3 minutes. Drain and refresh in cold water. Slip the tender beans from their skins and set aside.

Add a splash of oil to a large, deep-sided frying pan over medium heat. Add the garlic and cook for 1 minute until fragrant. Add the broad beans and peas and warm through for a minute or so. Add a splash of white wine and cook until the wine has evaporated. Add the cream and butter, stir and cook until the butter has melted and the sauce is bubbling. Season with salt and pepper and take off the heat.

Tip the broad bean mix into a serving dish, scatter over the mint leaves and jamon and serve.

SERVES 6

5 cups podded broad beans
extra virgin olive oil
3 garlic cloves, finely sliced
250 g fresh or frozen peas
splash of dry white wine
120 ml cream
50 g butter
salt flakes and freshly ground black pepper
1 handful of mint leaves
6 slices of jamon (or prosciutto), torn

ROASTED CAULIFLOWER & PARSNIP WITH CUMIN, CHILLI & PARMESAN

This is a bit of an update on good old cauliflower cheese. Parsnip and cauliflower work really well together, especially when roasted with a hint of spice. This is perfect with roast pork, chicken or a leg of lamb.

Preheat the oven to 180°C fan-forced (200°C conventional). Line a large baking tray with baking paper.

Add the cauliflower and parsnip to a large bowl, drizzle with oil, sprinkle over the cumin, season with salt and pepper and toss gently to coat. Spread the vegetables out in one layer on the prepared tray and roast for 40 minutes.

Remove from the oven, drizzle with the cream, scatter over the cheese and sprinkle on the chilli powder. Return to the oven for a further 10 minutes until golden.

SERVES 6–8

1 head of cauliflower, cut into large florets
3 parsnips, sliced into 1-cm thick rounds
extra virgin olive oil
2 teaspoons ground cumin
salt flakes and freshly ground black pepper
3 tablespoons cream
60 g Grana Padano cheese, finely grated
1 teaspoon chilli powder

GRILLED EGGPLANT WITH TAHINI & YOGHURT DRESSING, POMEGRANATE, CHILLI & MINT

Eggplant, especially with a little char from the grill, loves Middle Eastern flavours. Serve with grilled meat or baked fish, or as part of a feast of mezze.

Preheat a griddle pan or barbecue grill until hot.

Slice the eggplant into 1.5-cm thick rounds, brush with oil and season. Grill for a few minutes on each side then lay flat to cool. The eggplant should be just cooked but still holding its shape.

Toast the cumin seeds in a dry frying pan until fragrant. Tip into a large mortar and grind coarsely. Add two good pinches of salt and grind roughly. Finely grate in the garlic, add the tahini, yoghurt, a good grind of pepper and the lemon juice and mix well.

Lay the eggplant on a serving plate, spoon the dressing over the top and scatter over the mint, chilli and pomegranate seeds. Drizzle with oil and serve.

SERVES 6

3 large eggplants, peeled lengthways leaving alternating stripes of skin on
extra virgin olive oil
salt flakes and freshly ground black pepper
2 teaspoons cumin seeds
2 garlic cloves
2 tablespoons tahini
300 g thick plain yoghurt
juice of 1 lemon
¼ bunch of mint, leaves picked
½ long green chilli, sliced
½ long red chilli, sliced
seeds of ½ pomegranate

BROCCOLINI WITH BACON, SHALLOTS, GARLIC & CHILLI

This is such a tasty vegetable dish and goes with anything from grilled meats to simple roast chicken and fish.

Cook the broccolini in a large saucepan of boiling salted water for 4–5 minutes until just tender. Drain but reserve a little of the cooking water.

While the broccolini cooks, fry the bacon for 3–4 minutes in a large frying pan over high heat – you shouldn't need oil at this stage, as fat will render out of the bacon. When the bacon starts to brown, add the oil, shallots and garlic and cook for 3 minutes, or until the garlic is fragrant and the onion has softened and started to take on some colour. Add the hot broccolini, chilli flakes and a splash of the reserved cooking water to the pan. Toss through for another minute or so, reducing the liquid and coating the broccolini well.

Pile into a serving bowl with all of the pan juices. Finely grate over the parmesan and serve.

SERVES 4

3 bunches of broccolini, trimmed and stalks cut in half on an angle
150 g bacon, sliced into lardons
2½ tablespoons extra virgin olive oil
3 French shallots, thickly sliced
3 large garlic cloves, sliced
1 teaspoon dried chilli flakes
40 g Grana Padano cheese

ROASTED CARROTS WITH RAISINS, HARISSA & CORIANDER

Cooking the carrots in butter really elevates their flavour. Their richness, along with the sweet raisins and currants, is offset by the fiery intensity of the fresh harissa. Serve with roast beef or baked fish.

Preheat the oven to 160°C fan-forced (180°C conventional).

For the harissa, place the whole garlic bulb, capsicum and chillies in a baking dish and coat with oil. Roast for 20 minutes. Remove the chillies and place in a medium bowl. Cover with plastic wrap and set aside for 10 minutes. Continue roasting the garlic and capsicum for a further 10 minutes. Place the cooked capsicum in a medium bowl, cover with plastic wrap and set aside for 10 minutes. Set the garlic aside. Peel and core the chillies and capsicum and scrape out the seeds. Toast the cumin and caraway seeds in a dry frying pan over high heat for 1 minute while shaking the pan constantly. Tip the spices into a mortar and grind coarsely. Cut the top off the garlic bulb and squeeze the pulp into the bowl of a food processor. Add the capsicum and chilli flesh, ground spices, passata, tomato paste, salt, sugar and 55 ml of oil and process until smooth.

Turn the oven up to 170°C fan-forced (190°C conventional).

Add the currants, raisins and vinegar to a small saucepan and simmer for 2 minutes.

Place the carrots in a large ceramic baking dish that fits them loosely. Drizzle with a little oil and season with salt and pepper. Roughly distribute the butter over the carrots and scatter over the cumin. Pour 100 ml of hot water into the dish, cover with foil and roast for 20 minutes.

After 20 minutes, remove the foil and scatter over the raisins and currants along with any vinegar. Continue roasting, shaking the tray occasionally, until the carrots are cooked (another 20 minutes or so). Remove from the oven and allow to cool a little before serving.

Dollop about 4 tablespoons of harissa onto the carrots, scatter over the coriander and serve. The remaining harissa will keep in the fridge for up to 5 days.

SERVES 6

30 g currants
30 g fat golden raisins
100 ml red wine vinegar
2 bunches of Dutch or Chantenay carrots, scrubbed and trimmed with large carrots split in half
extra virgin olive oil
salt flakes and freshly ground black pepper
2 knobs of butter
2 teaspoons cumin seeds
4 coriander sprigs, leaves picked

HARISSA

1 garlic bulb
1 large red capsicum
5 long red chillies
55 ml extra virgin olive oil, plus extra
3 teaspoons cumin seeds
3 teaspoons caraway seeds
100 ml passata
1 tablespoon tomato paste
1 tablespoon salt flakes
2 teaspoons caster sugar

TIP

If you don't have time to make your own harissa, you can use a store-bought one, but make sure you adjust the serving quantity to taste as they are usually quite fiery. My harissa recipe will make more than you need, but it keeps well in the fridge and can be used to accompany so many dishes. Serve it with fried chicken or lamb sausages, stir it through soups such as Spiced Lentil and Potato (see page 69) for a little chilli kick, or dollop it on top of an omelette or any fish dish (it's delicious with Baked Blue-eye and Prawn Parcels, see page 141).

SPICED PUMPKIN & SWEET POTATO BAKE WITH PICKLED ONION & HALOUMI

Putting pickled onions in a vegetable bake may seem a little unusual at first, but their sweetness and vinegary tang is a great foil for the spiced vegetables and salty haloumi. This is a really versatile side, try it with roasted meat or poultry.

Preheat the oven to 180°C fan-forced (200°C conventional). Line two baking trays with baking paper.

Place the sliced pumpkin and potato on the prepared trays, drizzle with oil, season with salt and pepper and dust with the cinnamon and allspice. Bake for 20–25 minutes until tender.

In a medium baking dish, add a layer of pumpkin and sweet potato, a bay leaf, some onion and haloumi, spoon over some cream and repeat until finished. You are not trying to make even layers here, more of an irregular stack. Cover with foil and bake for 15 minutes, then bake uncovered for another 10 minutes until golden.

Once cooked, squeeze a good amount of lemon over the top and serve.

SERVES 4–6

1 kg Kent pumpkin, cut into 1-cm thick slices
2 white sweet potatoes, cut into 1-cm thick slices
extra virgin olive oil
salt flakes and freshly ground black pepper
1 teaspoon ground cinnamon
1 teaspoon ground allspice
4 fresh bay leaves
15 small pickled onions, cut in half
1 × 250 g packet of haloumi, thinly sliced
100 ml cream
1 lemon

RATATOUILLE

Ratatouille recipes vary from the super-refined to the super-rustic. I like to keep mine pretty rustic, with chunky and textural vegetables, and add an underlying note of orange. Eat this as a warm side dish, or on bruschetta with ricotta, mozzarella or goat's curd. It also makes for a delicious breakfast with Baked Eggs (see page 26).

Preheat the oven to 180°C fan-forced (200°C conventional).

Place the eggplants on a baking tray and bake for 60 minutes. Set aside to cool. Once cooled, cut the eggplants in half, scoop out the flesh and chop roughly.

Scorch the skins of the capsicums over a gas burner, blackening them all over – you can also place them under a hot grill. Once blackened, place in a large bowl, cover with plastic wrap and set aside for 10–15 minutes to sweat and cool. Peel, core and deseed. Cut the flesh into 3-cm squares.

Add the oil to a medium saucepan over medium heat. Add the onion and garlic, stir and cook for 5 minutes until softened and fragrant. Add the bay leaves and oregano and cook for a further 5 minutes. Add the capsicum and cook for 10 minutes, stirring frequently. Add the zucchini, eggplant, tomato, tomato paste, orange zest and juice, and sugar, season with salt and pepper and simmer gently for 35 minutes, or until the zucchini is tender but still holding its shape. The mix will be quite stiff to start with, but the zucchini will let out quite a bit of water as it cooks, so watch it carefully.

To serve, squeeze in some lemon juice and adjust the seasoning if necessary.

SERVES 6–8

2 large eggplants, pierced with a fork
3 red capsicums
150 ml extra virgin olive oil
1 large brown onion, sliced in half moons
4 garlic cloves, finely chopped
2 fresh bay leaves
2 tablespoons dried oregano
5 small zucchini, cut into 3-cm rounds
½ × 400 g can chopped tomatoes
1 tablespoon tomato paste
finely grated zest of ½ orange
juice of 1 orange
2 teaspoons brown sugar
salt flakes and freshly ground black pepper
lemon juice, to taste

PASTA *and* RICE

BARLEY 'RISOTTO' WITH PINE MUSHROOMS & PANCETTA 112

'ARROZ CAMPERO' WITH PRAWNS, CALAMARI & MUSSELS 114

SPAGHETTI WITH SPINACH, CURRANTS, PINE NUTS, CHILLI & MINT 117

GOLDEN BAKED PASTA WITH CAULIFLOWER & CHEESE 118

ORECCHIETTE WITH TUNA, SPINACH, MASCARPONE & LEMON 120

ORZO WITH PRAWNS & FENNEL 123

PENNETTE WITH SMOKED TROUT, CRÈME FRAÎCHE, SPINACH & PANCETTA 124

RIGATONI BOLOGNESE WITH PEAS & BASIL 126

BARLEY 'RISOTTO' WITH PINE MUSHROOMS & PANCETTA

The meaty texture and nuttiness of pine mushrooms make them ideal for this 'risotto', and these days they're widely available when in season. Swiss browns also work well, as do king brown or field mushrooms. Don't use Asian funghi though, the flavour and texture just isn't right for the dish.

Bring 1 litre of water to the boil, add the barley and simmer for 15 minutes. Drain well.

Bring the chicken stock to a simmer in a saucepan and keep warm on low heat.

Heat a large, heavy-based saucepan over medium heat, add the pancetta and fry for around 5 minutes, or until the pancetta starts to crisp up and most of the fat renders off. Add 50 g of butter, the shallots and garlic and fry until softened. Add the thyme and mushrooms, season and cook until the mushrooms have softened. Add the barley and white wine and cook until the pan is almost dry. Add a few ladles of hot stock and stir until the barley takes up most of the liquid. Repeat this process of adding the stock like you would with risotto until the barley is cooked but still a little chewy – you don't need to be as precise as with risotto or stir as much, but adding the stock gradually makes it much easier to get the right consistency at the end.

Once the barley is cooked and the 'risotto' is still a little wet, take off the heat and stir in the grated cheese and a knob or two of butter if it needs enriching. Adjust the seasoning if necessary and serve immediately.

SERVES 4

250 g pearl barley
1 litre chicken stock
120 g pancetta slices, shredded
50 g butter, plus extra
3 large French shallots, finely diced
5 garlic cloves, finely chopped
3 thyme sprigs, leaves picked
350 g pine and/or Swiss brown mushrooms, cleaned, trimmed and sliced
salt flakes and freshly ground black pepper
100 ml dry white wine
60 g Grana Padano cheese, finely grated

'ARROZ CAMPERO' WITH PRAWNS, CALAMARI & MUSSELS

This is a Spanish-style rice dish similar to paella. It can be difficult to make a perfect paella at home, as it's hard to get even heat across a large pan without stirring the rice. This has the same sense of celebration and community about it, generous, robust and delicious.

Bring the stock to a simmer in a saucepan over medium heat, stir through the tomato paste until it dissolves, then reduce the heat to low to keep warm.

Dry the calamari well with paper towel. Cut the hoods into 3-cm rings with the wings still attached. Cut the tentacles into sets of two each, trim into manageable lengths and set aside.

Heat the oil in a large, deep-sided frying pan over medium–high heat. Add the chorizo and fry quickly until crisping up. Add the onion, garlic, capsicum, chilli, paprika and cayenne and cook for 5–7 minutes until the vegetables have softened and are starting to caramelise. Remove from the pan and set aside.

Sear the calamari and prawns in the same pan, tossing through for 1 minute only. Remove from the pan, set aside and keep warm.

Return the chorizo and onion mixture to the pan with the rice, stir through to warm and coat the rice. Add the hot stock to the pan and stir through. Cook on high heat for 6 minutes before stirring through the prawns and calamari. Reduce the heat to low and tuck the mussels into the rice. Cook for a further 10 minutes, stirring occasionally.

Remove from the heat and cover with a tea towel or foil for 10 minutes. The residual heat and steam will finish cooking the rice.

To serve, scatter over some coriander or parsley leaves and serve in the pan with plenty of lemon wedges.

SERVES 8

1.5 litres chicken stock
2 tablespoons tomato paste
2 small–medium calamari, cleaned, wings attached and tentacles kept (about 400 g cleaned weight)
3 tablespoons extra virgin olive oil
150 g chorizo, sliced on an angle
2 large brown onions, finely diced
6 garlic cloves, sliced
2 red capsicums, deseeded and cut into 2.5-cm squares
3 long green chillies, deseeded and sliced
1½ teaspoons smoked paprika
1 teaspoon cayenne pepper
8 green king prawns, peeled and deveined with heads and tails intact
500 g calasparra or arborio rice
500 g mussels, scrubbed and de-bearded
1 handful of coriander or flat-leaf parsley leaves
lemon wedges, to serve

SPAGHETTI WITH SPINACH, CURRANTS, PINE NUTS, CHILLI & MINT

This is a bit of a riff on one of my favourite Sicilian pastas. I would normally pair these flavours with anchovies or sardines, but I also love them with the simple freshness of baby spinach.

Place the currants and vinegar in a small saucepan, bring to the boil and take off the heat. The currants will plump up in the vinegar as they sit.

Cook the pasta in plenty of boiling salted water until just al dente – keep the pasta on the firmer side, it will cook more in the sauce. Drain the pasta, reserving a little of the cooking water.

While the pasta cooks, add a generous splash of olive oil to a large, wide-based saucepan or deep-sided frying pan over high heat. Add the garlic and chilli and fry quickly until fragrant. Stir in the currants and vinegar and cook for 1 minute. Add the spinach, cook until wilted and season with salt and pepper. Add the stock and cream and bring to a simmer, cook for about 30 seconds and take off the heat.

Add the pasta to the pan with a splash of the pasta cooking water, bring back to a simmer and toss through. Add the pine nuts and simmer in the liquid for a minute or so, tossing through a few times. As the sauce reduces and emulsifies it will start to cling to the pasta, just add some more pasta water if it becomes too dry. Gloss with a splash of oil, throw in the mint, squeeze over some lemon juice, toss through and serve immediately.

SERVES 4

2 handfuls of currants
4 tablespoons sherry vinegar
500 g spaghetti
extra virgin olive oil
5 large garlic cloves, finely sliced
3 small red chillies, finely sliced
3 handfuls of baby spinach
salt flakes and freshly ground black pepper
150 ml chicken stock
100 ml double cream
100 g pine nuts, toasted
2 handfuls of mint leaves
½ lemon

GOLDEN BAKED PASTA WITH CAULIFLOWER & CHEESE

This dish came out of an attempt to convince my girls to eat cauliflower. It's now a midweek family favourite. It reheats well, or you could even assemble and freeze; just thaw on the bench for an hour or so before baking (it may take an extra 20 minutes to cook).

Preheat the oven to 180°C fan-forced (200°C conventional).

Cook the pasta in plenty of boiling salted water in a large saucepan. Tip the cauliflower in with the pasta for the last 5 minutes of cooking. Drain.

While the pasta cooks, add the butter to a medium saucepan and melt over medium heat. Add the onion and garlic, season and cook for around 4 minutes until fragrant and softened. Add the curry powder and fry off quickly until fragrant. Add the flour and stir through to cook out the raw flavour of the flour. Pour in the warm milk while whisking and cook for 2 minutes, whisking continuously. The sauce should have thickened and be free of lumps. Add the cream and both cheeses and whisk until combined. Season then tip into a large bowl with the pasta and cauliflower. Stir through, breaking up the larger pieces of cauliflower a little as you go.

Tip the pasta mix into a ceramic baking dish, top with the breadcrumbs and bake for 20–30 minutes until golden and bubbling.

SERVES 4–6

500 g conchiglie (shell) pasta
½ cauliflower, cut in 1-cm slices
90 g butter
1 red onion, finely diced
5 garlic cloves, finely sliced
salt flakes and freshly ground black pepper
2 tablespoons curry powder
90 g plain flour
1 litre milk, warmed
200 ml cream
100 g Grana Padano cheese, finely grated
100 g edam or cheddar, grated
1 handful of fresh breadcrumbs

ORECCHIETTE WITH TUNA, SPINACH, MASCARPONE & LEMON

I like a good spike of fennel seed and plenty of fresh lemon in tuna pasta. This particular recipe came out of a moment staring at an empty pantry and an even emptier fridge. There's always something though, and it's usually delicious.

Cook the pasta in plenty of boiling salted water until al dente. Drain the pasta, reserving a little of the cooking water.

While the pasta cooks, heat a good slug of oil in a large, deep-sided frying pan over high heat. Add the tomato, season and cook for 3 minutes. Add the garlic, chilli and fennel seeds, stir and cook for a couple of minutes until fragrant. Add the parsley and spinach and cook until wilted. Add the tuna, lemon zest and juice and take off the heat. Stir through, breaking up the tuna a little with your spoon.

Add the pasta to the pan with the mascarpone and a splash of the pasta cooking water, season and toss through over medium heat until the pasta is nicely coated. Dress with a splash more oil, toss through and serve in shallow bowls with a sprinkling of chilli flakes.

SERVES 4

500 g orecchiette
extra virgin olive oil
1 large tomato, diced
salt flakes and freshly ground black pepper
4 large garlic cloves, finely chopped
1 teaspoon dried chilli flakes, plus extra
1 teaspoon fennel seeds
½ bunch of flat-leaf parsley, leaves picked and roughly chopped
3 big handfuls of baby spinach
1 × 185 g can tuna in oil, drained
finely grated zest and juice of ½ lemon
3 heaped tablespoons mascarpone

ORZO WITH PRAWNS & FENNEL

I will never tire of the combination of prawns, fennel and tomato. Cooking the pasta like this (a bit like risotto) means it takes up so much flavour. I have used chicken stock to add an underlying richness to the dish, though you could definitely use fish stock if you prefer.

Heat the oil in a large, heavy-based saucepan over high heat. Add the tomatoes and fry for 2–3 minutes until softened but still holding their shape. Lift the tomatoes out and set aside.

Add the prawns and ground fennel to the pan, season and fry for 2 minutes. Lift from the pan, leaving most of the oil behind, and set aside with the tomatoes.

Add the garlic and diced fennel to the pan, season and cook on medium heat until lightly coloured and softened, about 6–8 minutes. Add the orzo, wine and stock, bring to a simmer and cook for 6 minutes, stirring frequently to stop it sticking. Add the prawns and tomatoes back to the pan and cook for another 3 minutes while stirring. Turn the heat off and stir through a knob of butter, cover and stand for 2 minutes.

To serve, scatter over the fennel fronds, squeeze over some lemon juice and take the pan straight to the table.

SERVES 4

100 ml extra virgin olive oil
6 tomatoes, cut in quarters (kumato tomatoes work well for this)
10 large green prawn cutlets, deveined with tails intact
1 teaspoon ground fennel
salt flakes and freshly ground black pepper
5 garlic cloves
½ fennel bulb, finely diced, fronds reserved for garnish
350 g orzo (risoni)
3 tablespoons dry white wine
1 litre hot chicken stock
1 large knob of butter
½ lemon

PENNETTE WITH SMOKED TROUT, CRÈME FRAÎCHE, SPINACH & PANCETTA

The crème fraîche gives this pasta a creamy richness with a pleasantly sour tang that matches the intensity of the trout and pancetta without being heavy. This is far from traditional, but it's pretty delicious.

Cook the pasta in plenty of boiling salted water until al dente. Drain, reserving some cooking water.

While the pasta cooks, heat a splash of oil in a large frying pan over medium heat. Add the pancetta slices and cook until crisp. Remove from the pan and set aside.

Add the shallots and garlic to the pan, stir and cook until softened and starting to pick up a little colour. Add the spinach and cook until wilted. Season and add the wine, bring to the boil, bubble for 1 minute and take off the heat.

Add the chunks of trout, the crème fraîche and about 3 tablespoons of the pasta cooking water to the pan and stir through gently, being careful not to break up the trout.

Add the pasta to the pan and toss through over medium heat. Add the parsley and toss through gently, keeping the trout in large pieces. Squeeze over the lemon, splash in a little oil, season with pepper (and salt if necessary, but keep in mind the pancetta will be added at the end) and toss through.

Serve in shallow bowls with the crisp pancetta pieces broken over the top and a sprinkling of dried chilli flakes.

SERVES 4

500 g pennette
extra virgin olive oil
10 slices of pancetta
4 French shallots, finely sliced
4 large garlic cloves, finely sliced
3 handfuls of baby spinach
salt flakes and freshly ground
    black pepper
100 ml dry white wine
250 g smoked trout, flaked
    in large pieces
200 g crème fraîche
2 handfuls of flat-leaf parsley
    leaves, torn
½ lemon
dried chilli flakes, to serve

RIGATONI BOLOGNESE WITH PEAS & BASIL

This version of the classic is less robust and hearty than some, but it has a silky richness with underlying notes of nutmeg and bay that I just love.

Add 100 ml of oil and the butter to a large heavy-based saucepan over medium heat. Add the onion and garlic, stir and cook for around 5 minutes until softened. Add the carrot, celery and celery leaves and cook, stirring frequently, for around 15 minutes until the vegetables are sticky and nicely caramelised. Add the pancetta, stir through and fry briefly. Add the mince by crumbling it into the pan gradually with your hands and stirring it through as it browns. Once all the meat is browned, add the wine and simmer for a couple of minutes, lifting any caramelised bits off the base of the pan with a wooden spoon. Once the liquid is almost gone, add the milk, bay leaves and nutmeg and season lightly. Reduce the liquid by two-thirds. Add the stock, tomato paste, tomatoes and a tomato can of water to the pan and cook over low heat for a further 2 hours or so.

Turn off the heat once the sauce has reduced and the flavours have melded and intensified. Adjust the seasoning if necessary. You can freeze the sauce once it has cooled, but letting a ragu like this stand in the fridge for a day or two really deepens and harmonises the flavours.

To serve, cook your pasta in plenty of boiling salted water until al dente. Warm half the sauce in a deep frying pan or large saucepan, add the peas and pasta, tear in the basil and toss through. Add a handful of cheese and a splash of olive oil, toss through again and serve with plenty of grated cheese on the side.

SERVES 4 (SAUCE SERVES 8)

100 ml extra virgin olive oil, plus extra
50 g butter
1 small brown onion, finely diced
4 garlic cloves, finely sliced
2 small carrots, finely diced
3 celery stalks, sliced and leaves chopped
100 g pancetta, finely diced
500 g pork or beef mince (or a mix of the two)
200 ml dry white wine
400 ml milk
2 fresh bay leaves
½ whole nutmeg, finely grated
salt flakes and freshly ground black pepper
500 ml chicken stock
2 tablespoons tomato paste
2 × 400 g cans crushed tomatoes
500 g rigatoni
100 g frozen peas
2 handfuls of basil leaves
Grana Padano, finely grated, to serve

FISH and SEAFOOD

GRILLED CALAMARI & PRAWNS WITH TOMATO, CHILLI, PARSLEY, MINT & MOGHRABIEH 130

TUNA PATTIES 132

BARBECUED FLATHEAD SANDWICH WITH ICEBERG, CORIANDER & SUMAC AIOLI 135

PAN-FRIED GARFISH WITH TARAMASALATA & SOUSED CUCUMBER, DILL & MINT SALAD 136

CURRIED RICE WITH EGG, SEARED SALMON, PEAS & SPRING ONION 138

BAKED BLUE-EYE & PRAWN PARCELS WITH POTATO, FENNEL & CHERMOULA 141

PAN-FRIED SALMON WITH ZUCCHINI FLOWERS, FRIED ZUCCHINI, CHILLI & MINT 142

PAN-ROASTED SNAPPER WITH GARLIC & BAY 144

GRILLED CALAMARI & PRAWNS WITH TOMATO, CHILLI, PARSLEY, MINT & MOGHRABIEH

The scent of grilled calamari is one of my all-time favourite aromas, but I love it even more when the hot squid hits this spicy herb and garlic paste. Make sure the squid and prawns are thoroughly coated in the dressing and pour every last drop over the salad.

Using a mortar and pestle, grind the garlic, dried chilli, fresh chilli, peppercorns and a pinch of salt to a rough paste. Add a little oil and the chopped herbs and grind to a paste. Add more oil to loosen, and adjust the seasoning if necessary.

In a medium bowl, toss the drained moghrabieh with the lemon juice and zest, season and pile onto a serving platter.

Mix the tomatoes with the remaining parsley leaves, onion and a splash of oil, season and pile on top of the moghrabieh.

Preheat the barbecue until very hot.

Lightly oil and season the prawns and calamari and grill until just cooked. The calamari will take about 2–3 minutes on each side and the prawns, depending on size, should only take 1 minute on each side.

Slice the calamari into 5-mm rings and add to a large bowl with the prawns. Add the herb paste and a squeeze of lemon and mix well. Adjust the seasoning if necessary.

Pile the seafood on top of the tomatoes along with all of the juices, scatter over the remaining mint leaves and serve with lemon wedges on the side.

SERVES 6

2 garlic cloves
2 teaspoons dried chilli flakes
1 small red chilli, sliced
1 teaspoon black peppercorns
salt flakes and freshly ground black pepper
extra virgin olive oil
½ bunch of flat-leaf parsley, leaves picked, reserve a handful of whole leaves and chop the rest
½ bunch of mint, leaves picked, reserve a handful of whole leaves and chop the rest
1½ cups moghrabieh (pearl couscous), simmered for 20 minutes and drained
finely grated zest and juice of 1 lemon
250 g cherry tomatoes, sliced in rounds
½ red onion, finely diced
200 g prawn cutlets, butterflied
2–3 medium calamari, cleaned, wings attached and tentacles kept (350 g cleaned weight)
2 lemons, to serve

TUNA PATTIES

I grew up eating tuna patties, and my girls love them as much as I did. They're also healthy, really economical and mostly made up of kitchen and pantry staples.

To make the patties, add the tuna to the bowl of a food processor and process until smooth. Add the lemon zest, parsley, 1 egg and 5 splashes of Tabasco and process. Add the potato and process until just combined.

Tip the tuna mix into a large bowl. Add the spring onion and 3 tablespoons of breadcrumbs and combine. Shape into small patties about 6 cm in diameter.

Beat the remaining egg and tip the breadcrumbs and flour onto separate plates.

Dip the patties in the flour, shake off any excess and dip in the egg, and then in the breadcrumbs, coating well.

Heat 2 cm of oil in a large, non-stick frying pan until hot and fry the patties for 2 minutes on each side until golden. Drain on paper towel.

Serve the patties with shredded iceberg, lemon wedges and a dollop of mayonnaise.

MAKES APPROXIMATELY 12 PATTIES

2 × 185 g cans tuna in spring water, drained
finely grated zest of ½ lemon
2 handfuls of flat-leaf parsley, leaves, chopped
3 eggs
Tabasco sauce
500 g potatoes, peeled, boiled and mashed
5 spring onions, sliced
4 cups fresh breadcrumbs
¾ cup plain flour
olive oil, for frying
shredded iceberg lettuce, to serve
lemon wedges, to serve
mayonnaise, to serve

BARBECUED FLATHEAD SANDWICH WITH ICEBERG, CORIANDER & SUMAC AIOLI

The inspiration for this comes from a brilliantly simple stand-up lunch at a popular Melbourne market. $9 very well spent. This is my version.

Preheat the barbecue on medium–high heat.

Add the sumac, lemon zest and juice and aioli to a medium bowl, combine and set aside.

Toast the bread on both sides on the barbecue grill.

Season the fish fillets with salt and pepper and dust with flour. Add a little oil to the barbecue grill, shake the excess flour from the fish and cook for around 2 minutes on each side until just cooked.

To assemble, spread each side of the bread generously with the aioli, add the onion, lettuce, fish and coriander, sprinkle over some extra sumac and serve immediately.

SERVES 4

1 teaspoon sumac, plus extra
finely grated zest and juice of ½ lemon
1 cup aioli
4 individual Turkish loaves, sliced in half horizontally
500 g flathead fillets
salt flakes and freshly ground black pepper
plain flour, for dusting
olive oil
1 small red onion, finely diced
¼ iceberg lettuce, leaves torn
¼ bunch of coriander, leaves picked along with the fine stems

PAN-FRIED GARFISH WITH TARAMASALATA & SOUSED CUCUMBER, DILL & MINT SALAD

Choose small and beautifully fresh garfish for this Greek-inspired dish. The finely textured flesh is so sweetly delicious and it cooks in a flash. This dish says summer to me.

Slice the cucumbers in rounds just under 1-cm thick and place in a large bowl. Add the lemon zest and flesh, chilli, dill, mint, sugar, extra virgin oil, 1 tablespoon of salt flakes and a good grind of pepper. Toss gently to combine and set aside for 15 minutes.

Heat 3–4 cm of oil in a large, deep-sided frying pan. Dust the fish in the flour, shake off any excess and carefully add to the pan. Cook for about 1½–2 minutes on each side until just cooked. Drain on paper towel and season.

Tip the cucumber salad into a serving bowl and scatter over the dried olives.

Serve the garfish with the cucumber salad, taramasalata and lemon wedges on the side.

SERVES 4

4 Lebanese cucumbers, peeled lengthways leaving alternating stripes of skin on
finely grated zest of ½ lemon
flesh of 1 lemon, chopped
1 long green chilli, finely sliced
1 handful of dill fronds
3 mint sprigs, leaves picked
1 tablespoon sugar
2 tablespoons extra virgin olive oil
salt flakes and freshly ground black pepper
olive oil, for shallow frying
8 small garfish, cleaned and scaled
2 tablespoons plain flour, seasoned
dried olives, to serve
250 g taramasalata
lemon wedges, to serve

CURRIED RICE WITH EGG, SEARED SALMON, PEAS & SPRING ONION

This is a really quick and tasty midweek meal that relies more on the pantry than the market.

Slice the salmon fillet into three strips lengthways, then cut each slice into three chunks, giving you nine similar-sized pieces.

Place a deep-sided frying pan with a tight-fitting lid over medium heat. Add the rice, cumin and curry powder and quickly heat while stirring. Add the boiling water, season and stir. Cover tightly, reduce the heat to low and cook for 7 minutes.

Add the eggs and melted butter to a small bowl, season with salt and pepper and whisk.

After the rice has been cooking for 7 minutes, take the lid off and fluff the grains with a fork. Pour the egg mix over the top, put the lid back on and cook for 4 minutes. Turn the heat off and stand for 5 minutes with the lid on.

Heat a medium, non-stick frying pan over high heat. Toss the fish in a splash of oil, season with salt and pepper and cook skin-side down for 1 minute. Toss the fish and continue to cook for another minute. Remove from the pan.

Add the salmon to a medium bowl with the peas, spring onion and coriander, squeeze in some lemon juice and toss gently.

Pile the salmon mix on top of the rice, sprinkle over some fried shallots and serve with plain yoghurt (if using).

SERVES 2–4

300 g salmon (or ocean trout) fillet, skin on
250 g basmati rice
1 teaspoon cumin seeds
2 teaspoons curry powder
650 ml boiling water
salt flakes and freshly ground black pepper
3 eggs
60 g butter, melted
extra virgin olive oil, for frying
¾ cup frozen peas, thawed under hot water
6 spring onions, finely sliced
1 handful of coriander leaves
½ lemon
fried shallots, to serve
plain yoghurt, to serve (optional)

BAKED BLUE-EYE & PRAWN PARCELS WITH POTATO, FENNEL & CHERMOULA

I picked up this chermoula recipe on an amazing, but far too brief, holiday in Morocco. Chermoula is great with vegetables, poultry and lamb, but really comes into its own with seafood. Cooking fish like this steams it gently in the fragrant herbs and spices and traps in all the beautiful juices.

Preheat the oven to 180°C fan-forced (200°C conventional). Line a baking tray with baking paper.

Boil the potatoes in salted water until quite tender. Drain and slice into 2-cm discs. Don't worry if they fall apart.

To make the chermoula, roughly pick the parsley and coriander leaves along with some of the finer stems. Chop until reasonably fine, but still with some texture, and add to a medium bowl. Add the salt, pepper and spices to the herbs, finely grate in the garlic and turmeric and combine. Add a splash of water and enough oil to loosen. Add the lemon juice and mix.

Add the fennel, leek and tomatoes to the prepared tray, drizzle with oil, season with salt and pepper and roast for 20 minutes. Set aside to cool.

Turn the oven up to 200°C fan-forced (220°C conventional).

Add the fish and prawns to a large bowl with half of the chermoula, toss to thoroughly coat and set aside for 5 minutes.

Tear off six 60-cm sheets of baking paper and lay them out on your bench. Place some of the potatoes in the centre of each and follow with the fennel, leek, fish, prawns and sliced lemon. Squeeze over the juice and flesh from the roasted tomatoes and spoon over some more chermoula. Brush the edges of the paper with the egg white, fold over and roll up tightly in half moon shaped parcels.

Place the parcels on a baking tray and bake for 12 minutes. Remove from the oven and rest for 2 minutes. Serve immediately, allowing guests to cut open their own parcel. This dish is delicious with a little fresh harissa served on the side.

SERVES 6

6 desiree potatoes, peeled
1 large fennel bulb, sliced into 2-cm thick wedges
1 leek, white and pale green parts, sliced in 3-cm rings
4 tomatoes, cut in half
extra virgin olive oil
salt flakes and freshly ground black pepper
6 × 150 g blue-eye trevalla fillets, skin left on
12 green prawns, peeled and deveined with heads and tails intact
½ lemon, sliced
1 egg white
Harissa (see page 104), to serve

CHERMOULA
½ bunch of flat-leaf parsley
½ bunch of coriander
½ tablespoon salt flakes
¼ teaspoon freshly ground black pepper
1½ tablespoons sweet paprika
½ tablespoon ground cumin
½ tablespoon ground coriander
6 small garlic cloves
30 g fresh turmeric (or 1 teaspoon ground turmeric)
extra virgin olive oil
juice of 1 lemon

PAN-FRIED SALMON WITH ZUCCHINI FLOWERS, FRIED ZUCCHINI, CHILLI & MINT

Zucchini, mint, chilli and lemon is such a classic combination that works beautifully with rare salmon.

Trim the zucchini flowers and remove the stamen. Tear the flowers in half and place in a medium bowl. Slice the baby zucchini in half.

Add the olive oil to a medium frying pan over medium heat and heat for 1 minute. Add the half moons of zucchini and fry until golden. Drain on paper towel briefly and add to the bowl with the flowers (the warmth of the zucchini will wilt the flowers).

Fry the baby zucchini until golden, drain and add to the bowl along with the chilli and half of the mint, season, toss gently and set aside.

Tip out most of the oil from the pan and turn the heat to high. Season the salmon pieces and cook on each side for 30–60 seconds, or until golden but still rare in the middle.

Place two pieces of salmon on each plate. Squeeze some lemon into the zucchini mix and toss through, pile on top of the salmon, scatter over the remaining mint, drizzle with a little extra virgin olive oil and serve.

SERVES 4

8 zucchini flowers with baby zucchini attached
150 ml olive oil, for shallow frying
4 small zucchini, cut into 1-cm thick half moons
1 small red chilli, sliced
1 handful of mint leaves, torn
salt flakes and freshly ground black pepper
4 × 200 g thick salmon fillets, skin on, cut in half lengthways
lemon wedges, to serve
extra virgin olive oil

PAN-ROASTED SNAPPER WITH GARLIC & BAY

Fish cooked on the bone is just so succulent and full of flavour. Keeping it simple is the real key. The garlic and bay perfume the snapper as it roasts. All that's needed is a good squeeze of lemon, a bowl of simply dressed leaves and some good bread to mop up the juices in the pan. Perfect.

Preheat the oven to 200°C fan-forced (220°C conventional).

Dry the fish inside and out with paper towel. Make an incision in the flesh on each side of each fish along the length of the spine. Splash on some oil, season with salt and pepper and rub all over, including inside the cavity.

Heat a large, ovenproof frying pan over high heat until hot. Add a good splash of oil and both snapper and cook for 2 minutes. Carefully flip the fish and cook for a further 2 minutes. Add the garlic and bay leaves to the pan and cook for a further minute until fragrant. Place the pan in the oven and roast for 8–10 minutes until the fish is just cooked.

Remove the pan from the oven and spoon some of the juices back over the fish. Squeeze over some lemon juice and spoon the juices back over a few times.

Serve immediately with some simply dressed green leaves and plenty of bread to mop up the juices.

SERVES 2

- 2 × 500–600 g snapper, cleaned and scaled
- extra virgin olive oil
- salt flakes and freshly ground black pepper
- 4 large garlic cloves, smashed, skin on
- 1 stick of fresh bay leaves with approximately 6–8 leaves attached
- 1 lemon

CHICKEN

- CHICKEN & CORN KOFTAS WITH AVOCADO & CORIANDER 148
- PAN-FRIED POUSSIN WITH BOIS BOUDRAN DRESSING 150
- BALINESE CHICKEN SATAY 153
- CHICKEN, OLIVE, LENTIL & RADICCHIO SALAD 154
- CHICKEN, KALE & MUSHROOM PIE 156
- BRAISED CHICKEN WITH WHITE WINE, SWISS BROWN MUSHROOMS, PANCETTA & THYME 159
- THE MR. WOLF CHICKEN SCHNITZEL & SLAW 160
- BAKED CHICKEN WITH SPICED RICE, CRANBERRIES & DILL 162
- ROAST CHICKEN WITH BUTTER, DILL & GARLIC ON A SOURDOUGH 'MATTRESS' 165

CHICKEN & CORN KOFTAS WITH AVOCADO & CORIANDER

This is such a perfect dish for summer entertaining.

Preheat the oven to 180°C fan-forced (200°C conventional). Preheat a griddle pan over high heat until very hot.

Brush the corn with a little oil and grill for 6–8 minutes, turning regularly. You want the corn to have lots of charred specks once cooked. Remove from the heat and, once cool enough to handle, shave the kernels off the cob with a sharp knife.

In a medium frying pan over medium heat, fry the onion, garlic, cumin, paprika and chilli powder in a little oil for 2–3 minutes until the onion has softened.

Add the onion mix to a large bowl with the corn kernels, breadcrumbs, chicken, chopped coriander, egg, ½ teaspoon of salt and a generous grind of black pepper. Mix with your hands until well combined. Wash and lightly oil your hands and roll egg-sized (approximately 70 g) portions of the mix into balls.

Heat a large frying pan over medium heat. Add a splash of oil and cook the koftas in batches for a couple of minutes on each side, flattening a little as they cook, until golden. Place on a baking tray and bake for 6–8 minutes until cooked.

Spread the avocado out on your serving platter, squeeze over some lime juice, scatter over the chilli and season with salt and pepper. Pile the koftas on top, scatter over some coriander leaves and serve.

MAKES 10–12

2 corn cobs
olive oil
1 large brown onion, finely diced
2 large garlic cloves, finely grated
3 teaspoons ground cumin
1 teaspoon smoked paprika
1 teaspoon chilli powder
1 cup fresh breadcrumbs
500 g chicken thigh mince
1 handful of coriander leaves, chopped, plus extra leaves to serve
1 egg, lightly whisked
salt flakes and freshly ground black pepper
2 ripe avocados, diced
1 long green chilli, thinly sliced
1 lime

PAN-FRIED POUSSIN WITH BOIS BOUDRAN DRESSING

The trick here is to let the just-cooked chicken rest in the dressing to soak up all the flavour. Perfect served warm as part of a feast.

For the Bois Boudran dressing, combine all the ingredients – add the Tabasco to taste, but I like about eight good shakes – in a medium bowl and set aside at room temperature for at least 20 minutes before using.

Preheat the oven to 180°C fan-forced (200°C conventional).

Season the poussin and dust with flour.

Add a good splash of oil to a large frying pan over medium heat and fry the poussin, skin-side down, for about 6 minutes until golden. Flip and cook for 2 minutes, then place on a baking tray and roast for about 6 minutes until just cooked.

Transfer the poussin to a serving platter, generously spoon over the dressing and rest for 20 minutes before serving.

SERVES 6

TIP
Bois Boudran dressing is also great with roasted or grilled quail; grilled whole fish, especially rich, oily fish like mackerel, tuna or sardines; or spooned over seared scallops or grilled prawns.

3 × 500–600 g poussin, butterflied and cut in half
salt flakes and freshly ground black pepper
150 g plain flour
extra virgin olive oil

BOIS BOUDRAN DRESSING
150 ml extra virgin olive oil
2½ tablespoons Champagne vinegar (or white wine vinegar)
100 ml tomato sauce
1½ tablespoons Worcestershire sauce
2 tomatoes, blanched, peeled, deseeded and finely diced
80 g finely diced French shallots (approximately 3 shallots)
1 large garlic clove, finely grated
½ bunch of chervil, leaves picked and chopped
½ bunch of chives, snipped
10 tarragon sprigs, leaves picked and chopped
Tabasco sauce, to taste

BALINESE CHICKEN SATAY

These fragrant satays are perfect for summer entertaining. The marinade caramelises as the satays cook, balancing the spice and punchy heat.

Soak a packet of wooden skewers in water for 20 minutes to prevent them from burning (or use metal skewers).

Place all of the marinade ingredients in a blender and process into a smooth paste.

Add the chicken and marinade to a large bowl and mix to thoroughly coat. Marinate for at least 1 hour, refrigerate for up to 24 hours.

When ready to cook, preheat the barbecue grill on high heat.

Thread the chicken strips on the skewers and cook for about 10 minutes, turning frequently. Only baste the chicken with the marinade the first couple of times you turn the skewers.

Once cooked, serve with steamed rice, sliced spring onion and chopped chilli.

SERVES 8–10

1.2 kg chicken thigh fillets, each fillet sliced into 4 strips
steamed rice, to serve
spring onions, sliced, to serve
small red chillies, chopped, to serve
lime cheeks, to serve

MARINADE

2 French shallots, sliced
4 garlic cloves, chopped
6-cm piece of ginger or galangal, finely sliced
3 lemongrass stems, white part only, finely sliced
3 small red chillies, finely sliced
1 teaspoon minced fresh turmeric (or 1 teaspoon ground turmeric)
2 tablespoons ground coriander
2 teaspoons ground cumin
2 tablespoons vegetable oil
3 tablespoons kecap manis
1½ tablespoons fish sauce
4 tablespoons brown sugar

CHICKEN, OLIVE, LENTIL & RADICCHIO SALAD

Lentils are a tasty and often overlooked salad ingredient. I first made this dish after a trip to Mount Zero Olives in the Grampians, where a friend of mine not only farms an amazing range of olives but also grows the most beautiful fine green lentils.

Cook the lentils in a saucepan of simmering water for 15–20 minutes until tender. Drain.

Dress the lentils in the vinaigrette and pile onto a serving platter.

Add the onion, lemon zest and juice, and a couple of pinches of salt to a small bowl. Mix through with your fingers and set aside for 10 minutes.

Add the almonds, olives, parsley, oregano and green chilli to a large bowl, drizzle with a little oil, grind in some pepper and toss through.

Heat a large, heavy-based frying pan over medium–high heat. Oil and season the chicken and add to the pan with the side that had the skin on it facing down. Cook for 6 minutes until nice and golden, flip and cook for about 2 minutes until cooked.

Cut each thigh into three and add to the almond and olive mix, toss to thoroughly coat.

Place the radicchio leaves on the lentils, pile on the chicken, scatter over the onion, spoon over any remaining almond and olive mix, grind over some pepper and serve.

SERVES 6

300 g green lentils
½ quantity French Vinaigrette (see page 74)
1 large red onion, finely sliced
finely grated zest and juice of 1 lemon
salt flakes and freshly ground black pepper
80 g blanched almonds, toasted and roughly chopped
140 g pitted olives (kalamata or green, but a mix is good), roughly chopped
2 handfuls of flat-leaf parsley leaves, finely chopped
½ bunch of oregano, leaves picked and finely chopped
2 long green chillies, sliced
extra virgin olive oil
800–900 g chicken thigh fillets
½ small head of radicchio, leaves torn

CHICKEN, KALE & MUSHROOM PIE

I really do love a good chicken pie and this is my favourite version yet. You can now buy beautiful all-butter puff pastry at the supermarket; it usually comes in one thick piece that you can carefully roll out to fit your dish. Almost as good as making your own.

Bring the stock to a simmer in a saucepan and blanch the kale for 1 minute. Remove the kale and use a sieve to squeeze any excess moisture back into the pan.

Oil and season the chicken thighs and cook, skin-side down, in a large deep-sided frying pan over medium heat for about 8 minutes until brown. Flip the chicken and add the hot stock. Simmer gently for 25 minutes until the thighs are cooked. Take off the heat.

Remove the cooked chicken and set aside. Strain the stock into a medium saucepan, return to the stove, skim off most of the fat and reduce to approximately 400 ml.

Preheat the oven to 190°C fan-forced (210°C conventional).

For the pie filling, add a good splash of oil to a large, deep-sided frying pan and cook the onion, garlic and leeks over medium–low heat for around 10 minutes until softened and starting to caramelise. Add the butter, mushrooms and thyme and cook for a further 5 minutes. Season with salt and pepper, add the flour and cook for 2 minutes while stirring. Add the strained stock and simmer for 2–3 minutes, stirring constantly. Stir in the double cream and mustard. Mix through the parsley and kale and take off the heat.

Pick the cooled chicken from the bones and tear or roughly chop the flesh. Add the chicken to the pan and gently combine. Adjust the seasoning if necessary.

Pick a baking dish that will fit the filling with only a small gap between the top of the mix and the lip – otherwise your pastry will sink and won't brown properly. Gently roll the pastry to fit the dish with a 3-cm overhang. Trim off any excess pastry, but keep the scraps. Brush the rim of the dish with the egg, tip the filling in and lay the pastry lid on top. Press the pastry down to seal and decorate the top with the scraps. Make a couple of incisions in the top to release steam and brush with the egg. Bake for 30–35 minutes until golden and puffed.

SERVES 4

- 4 stalks of kale, leaves stripped and roughly torn
- 1 litre chicken stock
- extra virgin olive oil
- salt flakes and freshly ground black pepper
- 1.5 kg chicken thighs, skin on and bone in
- ½ brown onion, finely diced
- 3 garlic cloves, finely chopped
- 2 leeks, white and pale green parts, finely sliced
- 50 g butter
- 450 g large pine or field mushrooms, cleaned and finely diced
- 3 thyme sprigs, leaves picked
- 40 g plain flour
- 2 tablespoons double cream
- 2 heaped teaspoons Dijon mustard
- 1 handful of flat-leaf parsley leaves, chopped
- 1 × 375 g packet of all butter puff pastry (1 thick piece)
- 1 egg, whisked

BRAISED CHICKEN WITH WHITE WINE, SWISS BROWN MUSHROOMS, PANCETTA & THYME

This is such a rustic wintery braise. Cooking the chicken on the bone adds so much flavour and keeps the meat succulent and moist.

Place the porcini in a small bowl and cover with boiling water. Set aside for 10 minutes to reconstitute. Reserve the liquid and roughly chop the flesh.

Add the thyme, bay leaves, a few grinds of pepper and a generous pinch of salt to a mortar and smash to a paste. Add a good splash of oil and mix, lifting the herbs from the mortar with a spoon, until you have a loose paste.

Add the chicken pieces to a large bowl and massage the herb paste into the meat.

Brown the chicken in a large, wide-based saucepan over medium heat – you want good deep colour on the chicken, but be careful not to burn the herbs. Season, remove from the pan and set aside.

Add the pancetta to the pan and fry until the fat starts to render out and the lardons brown and crisp up. Add the shallot and garlic, stir and cook for 5 minutes. Add the celery and carrot, season with a little salt and pepper and cook for 15 minutes, or until the vegetables are nicely caramelised. Add the chopped porcini and Swiss browns, stir and cook for around 5 minutes to soften. Add the chicken, wine and porcini liquid and simmer for 6 minutes. Add the stock, bring up to a simmer and cook very gently for 35 minutes until the meat is tender.

Remove the cooked chicken from the liquid and place in a serving dish. Reduce the braising liquid to your liking, adjust the seasoning if necessary, pour over the chicken and serve.

SERVES 4–6

15 g dried porcini
5 thyme sprigs, leaves picked
2 fresh bay leaves
salt flakes and freshly ground black pepper
extra virgin olive oil
1 × 1.6 kg chicken, cut into 8 pieces
5 thick slices of pancetta, sliced into lardons
5 French shallots, thickly sliced
8 garlic cloves, smashed, skin on
3 celery stalks, finely diced
1 carrot, finely diced
300 g small Swiss brown mushrooms, cut in half, tiny ones left whole
300 ml dry white wine
500 ml chicken stock

THE MR. WOLF CHICKEN SCHNITZEL & SLAW

There are a few secrets to making a great schnitzel: use the best free-range chicken; make your own breadcrumbs and keep them chunky; shallow fry to get an evenly golden crust; and match it with beautifully fresh slaw.

To prepare the schnitzel, cut each chicken fillet horizontally part way through the middle so that they each open out into one large piece. Place each fillet between two pieces of plastic wrap and beat lightly with a mallet or rolling pin to flatten out a little.

Combine the breadcrumbs, oregano, salt and lemon zest in a large shallow bowl.

Whisk the eggs in a bowl with the milk.

Tip the flour onto a plate and flour both sides of the chicken fillets. Shake off any excess flour and dip in the egg mix. Shake off any excess egg and place the chicken in the breadcrumbs, pressing the crumbs on to thoroughly coat. Set aside for 10 minutes at room temperature before cooking.

Preheat the oven to 180°C fan-forced (200°C conventional).

To make the coleslaw, mix the sour cream, mayonnaise, vinegar, oil, sugar and salt in a large bowl. Add the cabbage, apple, onion, carrot, radish and cheese and mix really well. Stand for 10–15 minutes for the flavours to develop.

To cook the schnitzels, heat some oil in a large, deep-sided frying pan over medium heat. Once hot, fry the chicken in batches for 2–3 minutes on each side until the crumbs are golden. Remove from the pan and drain on paper towel. Repeat until all the chicken is cooked. Place the schnitzels on a baking tray and bake for a further 5 minutes, or until cooked.

Serve the schnitzels with the coleslaw, a scattering of mint leaves and the lemon wedges on the side.

SERVES 4

4 chicken breast fillets
4 cups fresh breadcrumbs (made with stale bread)
1 tablespoon Greek-style dried oregano
1 tablespoon salt flakes
finely grated zest of 1 lemon
3 eggs
splash of milk
½ cup plain flour
200 ml olive oil, for frying
1 handful of mint leaves, torn
lemon wedges, to serve

SLAW

2 tablespoons sour cream (or plain yoghurt)
2 tablespoons mayonnaise
2 tablespoons white wine vinegar
2½ tablespoons extra virgin olive oil
1 tablespoon sugar
½ teaspoon salt flakes
½ small white cabbage, finely sliced
1 granny smith apple, finely sliced or coarsely grated
½ white salad onion, finely diced
2 carrots, finely sliced in ribbons or coarsely grated
4 red radishes, finely sliced
60 g Grana Padano cheese, finely grated

BAKED CHICKEN WITH SPICED RICE, CRANBERRIES & DILL

This dish has its origins in the Middle East. It reminds me of a dish my grandmother used to cook and is a bit like a version a friend makes, only spicier. It's also very similar to a dish that one of my favourite cooks, Yotam Ottolenghi, features in his book, Jerusalem. Whatever the origin, this is one of my favourite one-pot dishes.

Preheat the oven to 200°C fan-forced (220°C conventional).

Cover the cranberries with boiling water and set aside to rehydrate.

Add a good splash of oil to a deep-sided, ovenproof frying pan or flameproof baking dish over medium heat. Add the onion and garlic, season and cook, stirring occasionally, for about 15 minutes until caramelised. Tip into a bowl and set aside.

Bring the stock to a simmer in a saucepan and keep warm on low heat.

Wipe out the pan and return to the heat. Season the chicken thighs with salt and pepper and cook on each side for about 5 minutes until golden brown – enough fat should render out of the chicken, but add a splash of oil if the pan is too dry. Remove and set aside.

Tip most of the fat out of the pan and return to the heat. Add the rice, allspice, cardamom and a couple of pinches of salt and fry quickly until the spices are fragrant. Pour in the stock and spread half of the caramelised onion over the bottom of the pan. Add back the chicken, skin-side up, with the cinnamon stick and lemon zest and bring to a simmer. Distribute the remaining onion on top of the chicken pieces, pushing the thighs down so that they are mostly covered. Scatter over the cranberries and pumpkin seeds, cover tightly with foil and bake for 20 minutes.

Remove the chicken from the oven and rest for 5 minutes, covered. Remove the foil and fluff the rice with a fork, sprinkle over the chopped dill, squeeze over some lemon juice and serve with yoghurt.

SERVES 6

30 g dried cranberries
extra virgin olive oil
3 brown onions, finely sliced into half moons
4 garlic cloves, sliced
salt flakes and freshly ground black pepper
700 ml chicken stock
6 chicken thighs (approximately 1.4 kg), skin on and bone in
300 g basmati rice
1 teaspoon ground allspice
10 green cardamom pods, husks removed and seeds ground
1 cinnamon stick
peeled zest and juice of ½ lemon
1 large handful of pumpkin seeds
1 large handful of dill fronds, roughly chopped
plain yoghurt, to serve

ROAST CHICKEN WITH BUTTER, DILL & GARLIC ON A SOURDOUGH 'MATTRESS'

The idea for this recipe came from my fellow chef, Colin Fassnidge. The bread soaks up all the garlicky, herby, chicken-laced juices and is just so delicious. And yes, Colin my friend, mine is better.

Preheat the oven to 200°C fan-forced (220°C conventional).

Slice the top off the loaf so that you have a slab of bread 5–6-cm thick with the bottom crust still attached.

Season the chicken inside and out with salt and pepper. Cut the lemon into chunks and stuff inside the cavity with the thyme sprigs.

Using a mortar and pestle, smash the garlic with 1½ tablespoons of salt flakes until you have a paste. Add the butter, dill and a generous amount of pepper and combine.

Carefully separate the skin from the breast and legs of the chicken and place the butter under the skin. Distribute the butter evenly by smoothing down the skin.

Place the bread, crust down, in a roasting tray, add the bay leaves and sit the chicken on top. Drizzle with oil, season and roast for 40 minutes. Reduce the temperature to 150°C and roast for a further 40 minutes. Once the chicken is cooked, remove from the oven, cover with foil and rest for 10 minutes before carving.

To serve, carve the chicken while still in the tray to allow all the juices to seep into the bread. Tear the bread into chunks and serve with the chicken and juices from the tray.

SERVES 4

- 1 large loaf of quality sourdough (an oval loaf is ideal)
- 1 × 1.6 kg chicken, trimmed and dried with paper towel
- salt flakes and freshly ground black pepper
- ½ lemon
- 10 thyme sprigs
- 6 large garlic cloves
- 150 g butter, softened slightly
- 3 handfuls of dill fronds, chopped
- 2 fresh bay leaves
- extra virgin olive oil

MEAT

CIDER-BRAISED SMOKED BACON WITH APPLES & PRUNES 168

GREEK LAMB SHOULDER WITH YOGHURT, CUCUMBER & MINT 170

LAMB SHANKS BRAISED WITH BEER, HONEY & OREGANO 173

PORK & BEEF MEATLOAF WITH HALOUMI, PISTACHIOS & POMEGRANATE MOLASSES 174

BEEF MALTAGLIATA WITH ROCKET, RADICCHIO & RICOTTA 176

EGG NOODLES WITH SHREDDED BEEF, THAI BASIL & SESAME 179

BARBECUED MINUTE STEAK WITH ASIAN MUSHROOM DRESSING 180

BEEF RENDANG 182

RED-WINE BRAISED BEEF CHEEKS WITH CELERIAC & PARSNIP PUREE 185

SEARED RUMP STEAK WITH GREEN CHILLI & ANCHOVY MAYONNAISE & GREEN OLIVE SALAD 186

SEARED EYE FILLET WITH BEETROOT, GOAT'S CHEESE, BROWN BUTTER, CINNAMON & SAGE 188

ROASTED EYE FILLET WITH POTATO DAUPHINOISE & BAKED CAMEMBERT 191

CIDER-BRAISED SMOKED BACON WITH APPLES & PRUNES

This is such an intense and richly delicious dish. A small slice with a generous spoon of mash is perfect on a winter's day, but when the weather warms up it's just as good with some herby vinaigrette potatoes. A beautiful single piece of free-range bacon is essential.

Combine all the marinade ingredients in a large bowl and mix well.

Stud the underside of the bacon with the cloves and add to the marinade. Rub the bacon with the marinade, cover and place in the fridge overnight, turning occasionally.

When you are ready to cook, preheat the oven to 200°C fan-forced (220°C conventional).

Place the bacon in a flameproof baking dish, skin-side up, add the marinade, stock (don't immerse the skin in liquid as it won't colour) and whole apples and bring to a simmer on the stovetop. Cover with foil and bake for 45 minutes. Baste well with the juices, uncover and cook for 15–20 minutes, or until the bacon rind is a rich, dark tone.

Meanwhile, cook the potatoes in boiling salted water until tender. Drain well and rice or mash.

Gently warm the cream and butter in a saucepan until the butter melts. Stir through the mash until combined. Adjust the seasoning if necessary.

Remove the bacon and fruit from the baking dish. Place the dish over high heat and reduce until the sauce is slightly thickened and intensely flavoured.

Cut the bacon into slices about 2-cm thick and arrange on your plates along with the apples and prunes, spoon the sauce over the top and serve with the mash on the side.

SERVES 6

1 × 1.2 kg piece of smoked bacon, rind on
10 whole cloves
700 ml chicken stock
1.5 kg Dutch cream potatoes, peeled
200 ml cream
100 g butter
salt flakes and freshly ground black pepper

MARINADE
250 g dried apples
200 g prunes
500 ml apple cider
juice of 1 lemon
3 tablespoons honey
6 French shallots, thickly sliced
8 garlic cloves, smashed, skin on
1 cinnamon stick
2 teaspoons freshly ground black pepper
3 teaspoons ground ginger

GREEK LAMB SHOULDER WITH YOGHURT, CUCUMBER & MINT

This is possibly the fanciest souvlaki you'll ever eat. Slow-roasted lamb shoulder, in one form or another, is on constant rotation at home and I'm always playing with the recipe. It's all smiles in my house when this is on the menu. It really pays to make your own Pita (see page 42).

Preheat the oven to 160°C fan-forced (180°C conventional).

For the lamb, grind the salt, garlic and peppercorns in a mortar until you have a rough paste. Add the oil and oregano and mix well.

Rub the marinade all over the lamb, massaging it into the flesh vigorously. Place the lamb in a ceramic baking dish with the shoulder folded loosely back together. Add 125 ml of water and the vinegar to the dish. Cover with foil and roast for 3 hours, or until very tender.

Once cooked, remove the foil from the dish and increase the heat to 220°C with the oven grill on. Brown the meat for around 15 minutes until crisping up and nicely coloured. Remove from the oven.

For the salad, place the cucumber in a strainer, lightly sprinkle with salt and a little sugar and set aside for 10 minutes to draw out excess water. Combine the yoghurt, mint, lemon juice and garlic in a medium bowl and season with salt and pepper. Mix through half of the oil and stir through the drained cucumber. Tip into your serving bowl, dust with paprika and drizzle over the remaining oil.

To serve, break the lamb into large chunks and arrange on a platter, spoon over some of the pan juices and serve with the yoghurt dip, lemon wedges and flatbread.

SERVES 4–6

2 tablespoons salt flakes
6 garlic cloves, sliced
1 tablespoon black peppercorns
100 ml extra virgin olive oil
3 tablespoons Greek-style dried oregano
1 × 1.2–1.5 kg boned lamb shoulder
4 tablespoons white wine vinegar
lemon wedges, to serve
flatbread, to serve

YOGHURT, CUCUMBER & MINT SALAD

3 large Lebanese cucumbers, peeled, deseeded and cut into 1-cm dice
salt flakes and freshly ground black pepper
1 pinch of sugar
300 g thick Greek-style yoghurt
½ bunch of mint, leaves picked and chopped
juice of ½ lemon
2 garlic cloves, finely grated
1½ tablespoons extra virgin olive oil
2 teaspoons sweet paprika (or sumac)

LAMB SHANKS BRAISED WITH BEER, HONEY & OREGANO

This recipe is inspired by something I saw on a Rick Stein program. In the wild interior of Sardinia a woman filled battered roasting trays with lamb, beer and oregano and sealed them in an ancient wood oven for a couple of hours. The result was mesmerising, and apparently the best thing that Rick had ever eaten. This is my take with shanks.

Preheat the oven to 170°C fan-forced (190°C conventional).

Heat a heavy-based, ovenproof saucepan over medium heat. Rub the lamb shanks with oil, season with salt and pepper and rub the allspice into the meat. Brown the shanks in batches, turning them so that they brown gently all over without burning the spice. Remove the shanks from the pan and set aside.

Add a splash of oil to the pan with the shallots, garlic, celery, carrot and oregano, season and cook, stirring frequently, for 15 minutes. Return the shanks to the pot with the bones pointing up. Add the bay leaves, honey, beer and stock and simmer for 5 minutes.

Cover and place in the oven to bake for 1 hour. Uncover and cook for a further hour. The shanks are cooked when the meat is just pulling away from the bone. Reduce the sauce a little to thicken and adjust the seasoning if necessary.

Serve the shanks with mash, polenta or buttered risoni pasta and a generous ladle of sauce.

SERVES 8

8 lamb shanks, knuckles removed and French trimmed
extra virgin olive oil
salt flakes and freshly ground black pepper
3 teaspoons ground allspice
8 large French shallots, peeled and cut in half
10 garlic cloves, peeled and smashed
3 celery stalks, finely sliced
3 carrots, peeled and cut in chunks
3 tablespoons Greek-style dried oregano
4 fresh bay leaves
3 tablespoons honey
750 ml dark or other flavourful ale
800 ml chicken stock
mash, polenta or risoni, to serve

PORK & BEEF MEATLOAF WITH HALOUMI, PISTACHIOS & POMEGRANATE MOLASSES

A delicious midweek dinner and any leftovers are perfect for lunch. Serve a cold slice with a ploughman's lunch, or in a sandwich with a smear of sharp chutney.

Preheat the oven to 180°C fan-forced (200°C conventional).

Heat a good splash of oil in a large frying pan over medium heat and cook the onion and garlic for 2 minutes. Add the cinnamon and chilli, season with salt and pepper, stir and remove from the heat.

Add the mince, eggs, breadcrumbs and cooked onion mix to the bowl of a food processor and process until well combined. Tip into a large bowl with the oregano, haloumi and half the pistachios and combine.

Grease a loaf tin or baking dish with oil, spoon the mixture in, flatten down and top with the remaining pistachios. Cover with baking paper and foil and bake for 45 minutes.

Turn the oven grill on. Remove the paper and foil and pour the pomegranate molasses over the meatloaf. Cook for a further 10 minutes.

Remove from the oven and rest briefly before slicing and serving. This is delicious hot or cold.

SERVES 6

extra virgin olive oil
1 brown onion, finely chopped
6 garlic cloves, finely chopped
2 teaspoons ground cinnamon
2 teaspoons dried chilli flakes
salt flakes and freshly ground black pepper
400 g pork mince
400 g beef mince
2 eggs
1½ cups freshly made breadcrumbs
½ bunch of oregano, leaves picked and roughly chopped
1 × 250 g packet of haloumi, finely diced
100 g shelled pistachios
2 tablespoons pomegranate molasses

BEEF MALTAGLIATA WITH ROCKET, RADICCHIO & RICOTTA

This has been a mr. wolf menu staple for a decade. Any mix of pungent, coarsely textured leaves works well; in addition to rocket and radicchio you could also use curly endive, mizuna or even tatsoi. The peppery and bitter leaves balance beautifully against the caramelised beef, sweet balsamic and milky ricotta.

Arrange the rocket on your serving platter, follow with the radicchio, radish and half the parsley and basil. Drizzle over a little oil and some balsamic vinegar and season with salt and pepper.

Heat a large, non-stick frying pan over medium heat. Add a very generous splash of oil and heat. Toss the beef in the flour, shake off any excess and fry for around 3 minutes until golden brown. Season with salt and pepper, add the onion and remaining vinegar and stir to deglaze the pan.

Arrange the beef on the leaves and pour over all of the pan juices. Crumble over the ricotta, top with the remaining basil and parsley and serve immediately.

SERVES 4

3 handfuls of rocket
1 small head of radicchio, cut into small wedges
4 red radishes, finely sliced (slice tiny radishes in half but use a few extra)
1 handful of flat-leaf parsley leaves, torn
1 handful of basil leaves, torn
extra virgin olive oil
120 ml balsamic vinegar
salt flakes and freshly ground black pepper
600 g scotch fillet or rump steak, sliced into 1-cm thick strips
½ cup plain flour, seasoned
½ red onion, finely diced
200 g ricotta

EGG NOODLES WITH SHREDDED BEEF, THAI BASIL & SESAME

This is such a delicious midweek meal. Stir-fried beef works so well with plenty of garlic, ginger and sesame, and I love it with the aromatic anise notes of Thai basil. My girls love it too.

Add the soy sauce, sesame oil, sugar and pepper to a large bowl. Finely grate in half of the ginger and garlic and stir until the sugar dissolves. Add the beef to the marinade, mix through and set aside for 30 minutes.

Bring a large saucepan of water to the boil and blanch the gai lan for 1 minute. Lift out of the water and set aside. Blanch the noodles in the boiling water for 1 minute and refresh in cold water. Drain and set aside at room temperature.

Finely slice the rest of the garlic and ginger.

In a large wok over high heat, add the oil and heat for 1–2 minutes until just starting to shimmer. Add the sliced onion, garlic, ginger and sesame seeds and stir-fry for 2 minutes. Quickly spread the marinated beef around the wok in one layer and cook for 2 minutes without stirring. Add the spring onion and stir the beef through quickly. Add the noodles and gai lan and toss through for another 2 minutes until combined and hot. Add the rice wine, sizzle for a few seconds, then add the oyster sauce and toss through. Add the basil leaves, toss through again and serve immediately.

SERVES 4

- 2 tablespoons light soy sauce
- 2 teaspoons sesame oil
- 2 teaspoons white sugar
- 1 teaspoon ground white pepper
- 15-cm piece of ginger
- 6 garlic cloves
- 300 g eye fillet or scotch fillet, finely sliced
- 1 bunch of gai lan (Chinese broccoli), each stem sliced in half lengthways and cut in half
- 500 g fresh chow mein egg noodles
- 3½ tablespoons rice bran or vegetable oil
- ½ white onion, sliced
- 2 tablespoons sesame seeds
- 6 spring onions, cut into 5-cm batons
- 3 tablespoons shaoxing rice wine
- 3 tablespoons oyster sauce
- 2 handfuls of Thai basil leaves

BARBECUED MINUTE STEAK WITH ASIAN MUSHROOM DRESSING

Steak with mushroom sauce, but not as you know it! This dish is so well received whenever I cook it. It's an impressive looking plate of food but also just so quick to put together. Perfect for entertaining when time's not on your side.

Preheat the barbecue grill until very hot.

Oil and season the field mushrooms and grill for 3–4 minutes on each side.

Meanwhile, mix 2 tablespoons of olive oil with the oyster sauce, soy sauce, sesame oil, ginger, garlic and lemon juice in a large bowl. Add the raw mushrooms, chilli and most of the spring onion and toss through. Set aside while the field mushrooms finish cooking. The dressing will soften the mushrooms and infuse them with flavour, so make sure they sit for 5 minutes, or so.

Remove the cooked mushrooms from the grill, slice and add to the bowl of dressed mushrooms. Add a handful of coriander and toss through.

Lightly oil the steaks, season with salt and pepper and cook on the grill for 1 minute on each side.

Place the steaks on your plates and spoon over the mushrooms and dressing. Sprinkle over the remaining spring onions and coriander and serve immediately.

SERVES 4

4 large field mushrooms, cleaned and stalks trimmed
extra virgin olive oil
salt flakes and freshly ground black pepper
2 tablespoons oyster sauce
2 tablespoons light soy sauce
½ teaspoon sesame oil
8-cm piece of ginger, finely grated
2 small garlic cloves, finely grated
juice of ½ lemon
10 small shiitake mushrooms, sliced
1 × 100 g punnet enoki mushrooms, trimmed and separated
10 button mushrooms, cleaned and sliced
2 long red chillies, finely sliced on an angle
6 spring onions, finely sliced
2 large handfuls of coriander leaves
4 × 180 g scotch fillet steaks, beaten out between two pieces of plastic wrap to just under 1-cm thick

BEEF RENDANG

This is one of my absolute favourite curries. Traditionally it's quite a dry curry where there's just enough sweetly pungent sauce to coat the tender meat. The rendang really improves in flavour as it stands over a couple of days. It also freezes well.

Add the desiccated coconut to a dry frying pan over high heat and toss until toasted. Set aside.

Add the onion, garlic, chilli, ginger, galangal, turmeric, lemongrass, salt and a splash of water to a blender and blitz until you have a smooth paste.

Heat the oil in a large saucepan over high heat. Add the paste and stir until fragrant. Add the diced beef and stir until well coated with the paste. Add the shrimp paste and curry powder and cook for 2 minutes while stirring. Add the coconut cream, toasted coconut, sugar, lime leaves and 450 ml of water and bring up to a simmer. Reduce the heat and simmer slowly for 1½–2 hours, or until the beef is tender and starting to shred up and the sauce is quite reduced and starting to split. This is quite a dry curry, but if the meat isn't tender once the liquid has reduced, just add a little more water and cook down again.

To serve, stir the kecap manis through the rendang and serve with steamed rice and smashed chunks of chilled cucumber tossed with coriander leaves and a good squeeze of lime juice.

SERVES 6

90 g desiccated coconut
1 large red onion, roughly chopped
5 large garlic cloves, roughly chopped
6–8 small red chillies, roughly chopped
10-cm piece of ginger, roughly chopped
10-cm piece of galangal, roughly chopped
8-cm piece of fresh turmeric, roughly chopped
2 lemongrass stems, white part only, roughly chopped
2 teaspoons salt flakes
4 tablespoons vegetable oil or rice bran oil
1 kg beef topside or rump, cut into 3-cm dice
2 heaped teaspoons shrimp paste
2 tablespoons Malaysian curry powder
250 ml coconut cream
2 tablespoons brown sugar
6 fresh kaffir lime leaves
2 tablespoons kecap manis
steamed rice, to serve
chilled cucumber, to serve
coriander leaves, to serve
lime, to serve

RED-WINE BRAISED BEEF CHEEKS WITH CELERIAC & PARSNIP PUREE

This is one of my restaurant dishes that I've modified for the home kitchen. There's a little bit of work in this, but you can prepare it beforehand and warm when you're ready.

Preheat the oven to 155°C fan-forced (175°C conventional).

Heat a large, heavy-based ovenproof saucepan over medium heat. Add a good splash of oil and a couple of knobs of butter to the pan. Season the cheeks heavily and coat with flour. Shake the excess flour off the cheeks and brown in the pan, gradually adding more butter (about 50 g in total) as you turn them. You want a nice deep crust on the cheeks, but be careful not to burn them. Remove and set aside.

Wipe out the pan and add a splash of oil over medium heat. Add the onion, garlic, carrot, celery and leek and cook for 15–20 minutes, stirring frequently, until sticky and nicely caramelised. Add 3 star anise, the cinnamon, fennel seeds, bay leaves and thyme to the pan. Pour in the wine, keeping 100 ml aside to finish the sauce, and stir to deglaze. Bring up to a simmer and skim off any impurities. Add the beef cheeks back to the pan in one layer and cover with the beef stock. Seal with a tight-fitting lid or baking paper and foil and place in the oven for 3 hours.

Remove from the oven, uncover and set aside for 20 minutes before carefully transferring the cheeks to a plate. Cover the cheeks with plastic wrap and chill for 2 hours. This will 'set' the cheeks and make them easy to slice.

Strain the braising liquid into a jug and chill until a layer of fat forms on the top. Remove the fat and discard. Reserve two ladles of liquid and add the rest to a saucepan over medium heat. Add the remaining 100 ml of wine, a couple of sprigs of thyme and 1 star anise and reduce by at least two-thirds.

For the puree, place the celeriac and parsnip in a medium saucepan with the garlic, milk, a couple of pinches of salt and enough water to just cover. Cut a piece of baking paper to fit the inside of the pan and place on top of the liquid. Cook over a very low heat for 1 hour, or until the vegetables are very tender. Drain and transfer to a blender. Blend while gradually adding the butter and cream until you have a smooth puree. Season with salt and white pepper and keep warm.

To make the persillade, combine the ingredients in a small bowl.

To serve, slice each beef cheek into three and gently reheat in a deep-sided frying pan in the reserved liquid, about 2–3 minutes. Strain and reheat the sauce. Stir through 50 g of butter and mix until glossy. Adjust the seasoning if necessary. Spoon some puree onto each of your plates and add the sliced beef cheeks, draining off any of the warming liquid as you do. Spoon the sauce over the cheeks and finish with some persillade.

SERVES 4–6

---

extra virgin olive oil
100 g butter
1.5 kg trimmed beef cheeks
salt flakes and freshly ground black pepper
1 cup plain flour
2 brown onions, roughly diced
1 large garlic bulb, cloves separated and smashed, skin on
2 carrots, roughly diced
4 celery stalks, sliced
2 leeks, white and pale green parts, sliced in 2-cm rings
4 star anise
2 cinnamon sticks
3 teaspoons fennel seeds
3 fresh bay leaves
8 thyme sprigs, plus extra
750 ml decent full-bodied red wine
1 litre beef stock

CELERIAC & PARSNIP PUREE

1 large celeriac, peeled and chopped (650 g trimmed weight)
4 parsnips, peeled, cored and chopped (350 g trimmed weight)
3 garlic cloves
500 ml milk
salt flakes and ground white pepper
100 g butter
100 ml cream

PERSILLADE

2 large handfuls of flat-leaf parsley leaves, finely chopped
3 garlic cloves, finely grated
2 teaspoons fennel seeds, toasted and ground
100 ml extra virgin olive oil
salt flakes and freshly ground black pepper

SEARED RUMP STEAK WITH GREEN CHILLI & ANCHOVY MAYONNAISE & GREEN OLIVE SALAD

I was channelling vitello tonnato (the classic Italian dish of sliced veal with tuna mayonnaise) when I first made this. This is, pardon the pun, a beefed-up version, with ingredients that I just love together: green olives, anchovies, green chilli, mustard, lemon, orange, parsley and mint.

Preheat the barbecue or a griddle pan until very hot.

Oil the rump, season with salt and pepper and grill on each side for about 5 minutes – cooking time will depend on the thickness of the steak, but I'm aiming for medium-rare. Rest for 5 minutes before slicing.

While the rump cooks, combine the mayonnaise, yoghurt, anchovies, chilli, mustard and lemon juice in a small bowl. Adjust the seasoning if necessary.

Slice the rested rump into approximately 5-mm slices, place on your serving platter and smear with some of the chilli mayonnaise.

Mix the olives, herbs and orange zest with 3 tablespoons of oil in a medium bowl. Scatter over the meat and serve with the remaining chilli mayonnaise on the side.

SERVES 4–6

800 g rump steak (dry-aged if possible), at room temperature
extra virgin olive oil
salt flakes and freshly ground black pepper
½ cup mayonnaise
1 tablespoon thick plain yoghurt
4 quality anchovy fillets, chopped
3 long green chillies, finely chopped
2 teaspoons Dijon mustard
juice of ½ lemon
100 g pitted green olives, torn
5 mint sprigs, leaves picked
5 flat-leaf parsley stalks, leaves picked
finely grated zest of ½ orange

SEARED EYE FILLET WITH BEETROOT, GOAT'S CHEESE, BROWN BUTTER, CINNAMON & SAGE

The classic combination of beetroot and goat's cheese works so well with the rare beef and cinnamon-laced nut-brown butter. Make sure you take the butter to a hazelnut-skin colour (without burning) before stopping the cooking with lemon juice.

Preheat the oven to 180°C fan-forced (200°C conventional).

In a large bowl, drizzle the beetroot with oil, sprinkle over 1 teaspoon of cinnamon, season with salt and pepper and toss through to evenly coat. Wrap the beetroot in foil, place on a baking tray and bake for 1 hour, or until tender.

Once the beetroot is cooked, heat a large frying pan over high heat until very hot. Rub the steaks with oil, season with salt and pepper and cook for 3 minutes on each side. Remove the steaks from the pan, cover and rest for 5 minutes.

While the meat rests, add the butter to a small frying pan over medium heat. Once the butter has melted, add the sage leaves and cook until the sage is crisp and the butter has turned nut brown. Add a pinch of salt, the remaining cinnamon and a squeeze of lemon, stir and take off the heat.

To assemble, slice each steak in half horizontally, so that you have four thinner slices. Lay two slices of steak on each plate with the beetroot to the side, crumble over some goat's cheese and spoon the hot sage butter over and around the beef. Serve immediately.

SERVES 2

Ingredients:
- 1 large beetroot, scrubbed, topped and tailed and cut into thick wedges
- extra virgin olive oil
- 2 teaspoons ground cinnamon
- salt flakes and freshly ground black pepper
- 2 × 200 g eye fillet steaks, at room temperature
- 80 g butter
- 12–15 small sage leaves
- ½ lemon
- 600 g soft goat's cheese

ROASTED EYE FILLET WITH POTATO DAUPHINOISE & BAKED CAMEMBERT

Some people may think baking a round of camembert on top of a cream-laced dauphinoise is a bit decadent. And they're probably right. Well, they're almost definitely right, but this isn't exactly a midweek dinner. Reserve this for a special occasion and enjoy every bit of it, guilt-free.

Preheat the oven to 200°C fan-forced (220°C conventional).

To make the dauphinoise, rub the garlic on the base of a baking dish. I have used a 26 cm × 18 cm rectangular dish, but any shape is fine. Add the garlic halves, thyme, butter, cream and stock to a medium saucepan over low heat. Once the butter has melted, season with salt and pepper, stir and turn off the heat. Spoon some of the cream mixture into the dish, followed by an overlapping layer of potatoes. Season lightly and spoon over some more of the cream mix. Repeat, seasoning lightly every second layer, until you have used all of the potato. Spoon the last of the cream mix over the dauphinoise and seal tightly with baking paper and foil. Place the dish on a baking tray to catch any liquid oozing from the dauphinoise and bake on the bottom shelf of the oven for 1 hour.

When you are ready to cook the beef, heat a griddle pan or heavy, flat-bottomed frying pan over high heat until very hot. Rub the beef fillet with oil, season well with salt and pepper and massage into the flesh. Sear the fillet for 2 minutes on each of its four sides.

Place the branch of bay leaves in the base of a heavy baking dish, sit the beef on top and roast for 20 minutes. Remove from the oven, cover with foil and rest for 15–20 minutes before slicing.

After the dauphinoise has been in the oven for 1 hour, remove the paper and foil and bake for a further 10 minutes. Place the camembert on top, cut-side up, and cook for a further 10 minutes, or until the cheese is oozing and golden.

Remove from the oven and stand for 5 minutes before serving with the sliced beef.

SERVES 6

1 × 1.2 kg eye fillet (head end), removed from the fridge at least 1 hour before cooking
extra virgin olive oil
salt flakes and freshly ground black pepper
1 branch of bay leaves

DAUPHINOISE
1 large garlic clove, peeled and cut in half
5 thyme sprigs
100 g butter
220 ml thickened cream
400 ml chicken stock
salt flakes and freshly ground black pepper
4–5 large Dutch cream potatoes, peeled and sliced 2.5-mm thick with a knife or mandoline
1 small ripe camembert or brie, cut in half horizontally

DESSERTS

TOFFEED FIGS WITH CHOCOLATE PASTRY CREAM 194
PROSECCO JELLY WITH GRAPES, WHIPPED RICOTTA & CRUSHED AMARETTI BISCUITS 196
PEANUT BUTTER & BANANA ICE CREAM 199
LEMON SEMIFREDDO WITH BLACKBERRIES & LEMON SYRUP 200
CHOCOLATE RIPPLE & AMARETTI BISCUIT CAKE 202
APPLE & CHERRY TURNOVERS 205
FREE-FORM APPLE & BLUEBERRY TART 206
ROASTED PEACH & PEAR TARTS WITH VANILLA & THYME 208
MARTINI MESS 211
DELUXE MACADAMIA BROWNIE CAKE 212

TOFFEED FIGS WITH CHOCOLATE PASTRY CREAM

This recipe came about one day when I had some leftover pastry cream and plenty of Chocolate Brownie Biscuits (see page 233) on my hands. You only need about half of the pastry cream for this recipe, but it will keep in the fridge for five days for an encore performance, or use it to fill pastries. For something extra special, try it with my Mini Eclairs (see page 235).

To make the pastry cream, mix the custard and cocoa powders together. Add the yolks to a mixing bowl and whisk. Slowly rain the sugar into the yolks while whisking. Continue whisking for a few minutes until pale. Whisk in the custard powder and cocoa. Add the milk and mix until incorporated. Tip the mix into a medium saucepan and cook over low heat, stirring constantly with a wooden spoon, until substantially thickened. Swap the spoon for a whisk and whisk constantly, so as not to catch, and cook for a further 3–4 minutes. Take off the heat. Add the chocolate to the pan in two additions, whisking in until melted. Add the butter and whisk in, but not too vigorously, until incorporated. Pour into a container lined with plastic wrap, making sure to cover the top of the mix with plastic wrap to stop a skin forming. Refrigerate.

Fill a large bowl with cold water and set aside. Line a tray with baking paper with the shiny side facing up.

To make the toffee, add the sugar and 100 ml of water to a small saucepan and stir to combine. Place on high heat and cook for about 7 minutes until you have a light to medium caramel. Dip the base of the pan into the bowl of water to stop the cooking process. Remove the pan from the water.

Using a fork, dip the fig slices in the toffee to coat and place on the prepared tray. Set aside for the toffee to set. Don't leave for longer than 1 hour or the figs will start to weep.

Spoon or pipe a generous mound of pastry cream onto your plates, add the fig slices, top with the crushed brownie biscuits and finish with a dollop of crème fraîche.

SERVES 8

600 g caster sugar
8 ripe black figs, cut into 2-cm slices
Amber's Chocolate Brownie Biscuits (see page 233), crushed, to serve
8 heaped tablespoons crème fraîche (or sour cream)

CHOCOLATE PASTRY CREAM
50 g custard powder
25 g cocoa powder
70 g egg yolks (about 3–4 yolks)
80 g caster sugar
500 ml milk
30 g unsweetened dark chocolate (100% cocoa), finely chopped
170 g dark chocolate (70% cocoa), finely chopped
50 g unsalted butter

PROSECCO JELLY WITH GRAPES, WHIPPED RICOTTA & CRUSHED AMARETTI BISCUITS

Such a pretty little adult jelly. It's also a really easy dessert, and one you can prepare ahead of time and plate up in a flash.

Soak the gelatine sheets in cold water for 5 minutes.

Warm the prosecco and sugar in a medium saucepan over low heat. Stir until the sugar has dissolved and then take off the heat.

Squeeze any excess water from the gelatine before adding to the pan. Stir until the gelatine is completely dissolved and then strain.

Place the grapes in the base of eight dariole or small jelly moulds (you could also use larger decorative moulds) and divide the prosecco mixture evenly between them. Refrigerate, covered, for 4 hours to set.

To make the whipped ricotta, process the ricotta, sugar, lemon zest and juice in a food processor until smooth.

To serve, dip each mould in hot water for 5 seconds, shake gently and turn out onto your plates. Dollop on some whipped ricotta, sprinkle with the crushed amaretti biscuits and serve.

SERVES 8

10 gold-strength gelatine sheets
750 ml prosecco
200 g caster sugar
160 g small seedless grapes (blueberries would also work well), sliced
8 amaretti biscuits, crushed

WHIPPED RICOTTA
250 g ricotta
2 tablespoons caster sugar
finely grated zest and juice of ½ lemon

PEANUT BUTTER & BANANA ICE CREAM

This is a super-quick way to turn overripe bananas into delicious ice cream.

Add the banana, peanut butter and lemon juice to the bowl of a food processor and blitz for 30 seconds until smooth. Add the ice cream and process until smooth.

Tip half of the ice cream mix into a container large enough to take the whole mix. Top with a tablespoon of maple syrup and half the nuts. Add the rest of the ice cream and finish with the remaining maple syrup and nuts. Freeze for 1 hour before serving. If frozen for longer, soften a little in the fridge for 45–60 minutes before serving.

MAKES APPROXIMATELY 800 ML

3 large bananas, so overripe that the skins are black, peeled, cut in 4 and frozen (500 g peeled weight)
3 tablespoons smooth peanut butter
juice of ½ lemon
250 ml vanilla ice cream, slightly melted
2 tablespoons maple syrup
2 handfuls of salted roasted peanuts, crushed

LEMON SEMIFREDDO WITH BLACKBERRIES & LEMON SYRUP

This icy treat is just bursting with zesty citrus flavour. The semifreddo has all the refreshing qualities of a sorbet, making it a perfect after-dinner cleanser or afternoon treat on a hot day.

Line a 20 cm × 25 cm cake tin with plastic wrap – you could also use a loaf tin or terrine mould.

Finely grate the zest from 3 of the lemons and juice all 4 – you will need approximately 200 ml of juice. Mix the zest with the juice.

Beat the egg yolks and sugar with an electric mixer for 5 minutes until pale.

Add the yolk mix to a large stainless steel bowl and place over a saucepan with 5–6-cm of simmering water in it. Whisk continuously for about 5 minutes until considerably thickened. Take the bowl off the pan and whisk for 1 minute to cool down a little.

Add the lemon juice and zest to the bowl and whisk to combine.

Lightly whip the cream. Fold the double cream into the whipped cream and then fold this into the yolk and lemon mix.

Beat the egg whites with a pinch of salt until stiff peaks form. Fold through the lemon mix and pour into the prepared tin. Freeze for 6 hours or preferably overnight.

To make the lemon syrup, dissolve the sugar in 2½ tablespoons of water in a small saucepan over medium heat. Add the lemon zest and juice and bring up to a simmer. Take off the heat and chill for a couple of hours before using.

To serve, lightly mash some blackberries with a couple of tablespoons of syrup. Unmould the semifreddo and cut into thick slices. Serve with the berries and a drizzle of syrup.

SERVES 8

4 large lemons
4 extra-large eggs, separated
280 g caster sugar
250 ml cream
150 ml double cream
salt flakes
blackberries, to serve

LEMON SYRUP
100 g caster sugar
finely grated zest and juice of 1 lemon

CHOCOLATE RIPPLE & AMARETTI BISCUIT CAKE

My makeover of a nostalgic classic.

Whisk the cream, almond essence and vanilla with an electric mixer until stiff peaks form.

Spread a good layer of cream on one side of a chocolate biscuit and sandwich with another biscuit. Add more cream and biscuits until you have a barrel of seven biscuits. Repeat, making five barrels in total. Smear a little cream on your serving plate and line the barrels up side-by-side with some cream between each.

Repeat the process with the amaretti until they are the same length or a little shorter than the other barrels. You will need four of these. Smear some cream over the top of the cake and place the amaretti barrels in the dips between the chocolate biscuit barrels. Smooth a little cream over the top and tidy any edges. Refrigerate overnight to soften.

For the ganache, add the chocolate buttons and butter to a large stainless steel bowl over a saucepan with a few centimetres of barely simmering water in it. When two-thirds of the chocolate has melted, stir through twice and remove from the pan. Once the chocolate has fully melted, mix through the cream until evenly incorporated.

Pour the ganache over the top of the cake and smooth over. Smash some of the remaining biscuits and sprinkle over the ganache. Return to the fridge until ready to serve.

SERVES 6–8

600 ml cream
¼ teaspoon bitter almond essence
1 teaspoon vanilla extract
2 × 250 g packets of chocolate ripple biscuits
1 × 200 g packet of amaretti biscuits

CHOCOLATE GANACHE
300 g dark chocolate buttons (70% cocoa)
80 g unsalted butter
120 ml cream

APPLE & CHERRY TURNOVERS

These are at their best served warm with ice cream, cream or thick custard. They freeze well too; simply thaw for 15 minutes and bake. Perfect to have on hand for those dessert emergencies.

Chop the cherries roughly and add to a small bowl with the liqueur. Set aside for 30 minutes.

Add the sugar, honey, butter and apple to a large non-stick frying pan over medium heat and cook for 5 minutes. Stir through the cherries and liqueur and cook for a further 15 minutes, or until the fruit is soft and the liquid is quite reduced and sticky. Set aside to cool completely.

Preheat the oven to 200°C fan-forced (220°C conventional). Line a baking tray with baking paper.

Brush the edges of a pastry square with egg, add a heaped tablespoon of the cooled filling to the centre and fold one corner of the pastry over to the opposite corner, making a triangular parcel. Press the edges together and twist the corners to seal. Place on the prepared tray. Repeat until the pastry and filling are used up.

Brush the tops of the parcels with the egg and scatter over the flaked almonds. Bake for 20–25 minutes until golden. Dust with the icing sugar and serve.

MAKES 12–14

150 g dried cherries
100 ml cherry liqueur (or brandy)
70 g caster sugar
2 tablespoons honey
70 g unsalted butter
6 pink lady apples, peeled, cored and cut into 2-cm dice
3–4 puff pastry sheets, each sheet cut in 4
1 egg, whisked
2 tablespoons flaked almonds
pure icing sugar, to dust

FREE-FORM APPLE & BLUEBERRY TART

This rustic tart is ideal for keeping a crowd happy. Serve warm with plenty of cream or vanilla ice cream.

For the pastry, add the butter, sugar and eggs to the bowl of a food processor and process until smooth. Add the flour and pulse until the pastry comes together. Tip out onto a large piece of baking paper, place another sheet of baking paper on top and roll out to about 3-cm thick. Chill in the fridge for 30 minutes lying flat.

Preheat the oven to 180°C fan-forced (200°C conventional).

Bring the apple juice and sugar to the boil in a medium saucepan. Stir until the sugar dissolves. Add the blueberries and simmer for 2 minutes. Remove the pan from the heat, stir in the grated nutmeg, lemon zest and apples and set aside for 5 minutes.

Remove the chilled pastry from the fridge and roll out on the baking paper until about 2-cm thick. Lift the paper and pastry onto a baking tray.

Pile the fruit mix onto the middle of the pastry and, using the paper as support, pull the sides of the pastry up around and over the edges of the filling, leaving the middle open. Sprinkle with the extra sugar and bake for 45–55 minutes until golden with juices running from the tart.

Remove the tart from the oven, brush the juices back over the pastry and serve warm with ice cream or cream.

SERVES 6–8

---

100 ml apple juice
120 g raw sugar, plus 2 tablespoons extra
250 g blueberries
½ whole nutmeg, finely grated
finely grated zest of ½ lemon
2 × 400 g cans pie apples
ice cream or cream, to serve

SWEET PASTRY
250 g unsalted butter, at room temperature
150 g icing sugar
2 extra-large eggs
600 g plain flour

ROASTED PEACH & PEAR TARTS WITH VANILLA & THYME

These dainty little treats are surprisingly simple to make, and are delicious warm or at room temperature.

Add the dried peaches and pears to a bowl. Pour boiling water over to cover and stand for 30 minutes.

Preheat the oven to 200°C fan-forced (220°C conventional). Line a baking tray with baking paper.

Add the lemon zest and juice, sugar, vanilla, thyme and 250 ml of water to a medium saucepan and bring to the boil over medium heat. Add the drained fruit, cover, reduce the heat and poach for 15–20 minutes until tender. Lift the fruit out of the liquid and drain on paper towel. Reduce the liquid to a thick syrup.

Place the pastry sheets on a clean work surface. Lay the fruit on top, cut-side up, and cut out the pastry 2-cm wider than the fruit all the way around. Place the tarts on the prepared tray. Lift the fruit, prick the centre of each pastry shape with a fork a couple of times, then add the fruit back. Brush the edges with egg and bake for 10 minutes until golden. Remove from the oven, dust the pastry edges with icing sugar and bake for 3–5 minutes longer – this will glaze the pastry.

Serve the tarts with ice cream and a drizzle of the poaching syrup.

MAKES 10

---

5 dried peach halves
5 dried pear halves
finely grated zest and juice of 1 lemon
200 g caster sugar
1 vanilla bean, sliced on an angle
2 thyme sprigs
3 puff pastry sheets
1 egg, lightly beaten
pure icing sugar, to dust
vanilla ice cream, to serve

MARTINI MESS

This is the perfect dessert when you're catering for a big group. It has such a sense of occasion and drama about it; people always get so excited when you bring it out. Use the biggest platter you can find and go all out – this is one of the few times when keeping it simple is not the best strategy.

Choose your largest serving platter for this.

Smash the meringue into manageable pieces and scatter over the platter. Scoop the ice cream and distribute across the meringue. Scatter over the marshmallow cubes, prosecco jelly and raspberries. Sprinkle over some raspberry powder and serve immediately.

SERVES 10–15

1 quantity Meringue (see page 238)
500 ml vanilla ice cream
½ quantity Raspberry Sherbet Marshmallow (see page 243)
1 quantity Prosecco Jelly (see page 196), diced
250 g raspberries
freeze-dried raspberry powder, to serve

DELUXE MACADAMIA BROWNIE CAKE

The brownie cake is absolutely delicious in all its undressed glory, but it's just so glamorous smothered in ganache and decorated. It's perfect for a birthday or other special occasion.

Preheat the oven to 180°C fan-forced (200°C conventional). Butter and line a 26-cm springform cake tin.

Melt the chocolate and butter in a large stainless steel bowl over a saucepan with a few centimetres of barely simmering water in it. When two-thirds of the chocolate has melted, stir through lightly until combined. Take the bowl off the pan.

Add the eggs, caster sugar and vanilla to a large bowl and beat until light and fluffy. Add the flour and salt and combine. Add the macadamias and melted chocolate and fold through.

Pour the mixture into the prepared tin and bake for 20–25 minutes until the cake is firm to the touch. Allow the cake to cool in the tin completely before unmoulding and placing on a plate.

For the ganache, add the chocolate buttons and butter to a large stainless steel bowl over a saucepan with a few centimetres of barely simmering water in it. When two-thirds of the chocolate has melted, stir through twice and remove the bowl from the pan. Once the chocolate has fully melted, mix through the cream until evenly incorporated.

Gently skewer the top of the cake five or so times and slowly pour over the cherry liqueur. Spread the top and sides of the cake with the ganache, sit for 5 minutes and smooth on another layer of ganache. Decorate with morello cherries (if using) and gold leaf (if using). The cake can be served on its own or with a dollop of crème fraîche.

SERVES 6–8

- 180 g dark chocolate buttons (70% cocoa)
- 180 g unsalted butter, diced
- 3 extra-large eggs
- 200 g caster sugar
- 1 teaspoon vanilla extract
- 110 g plain flour
- ½ teaspoon salt flakes
- 180 g toasted macadamia nuts
- 1½ tablespoons cherry liqueur (or brandy)
- 8 morello cherries (optional)
- gold leaf, to decorate (optional)
- crème fraîche, to serve (optional)

CHOCOLATE GANACHE
- 300 g dark chocolate buttons (70% cocoa)
- 40 g unsalted butter, chopped
- 120 ml cream

CAKES, BISCUITS and SWEET TREATS

CARROT, PINEAPPLE & WALNUT MUFFINS WITH CREAM CHEESE ICING 216
RED VELVET CUPCAKES WITH MARSHMALLOW ICING 218
STICKY SEMOLINA CAKE WITH ALMONDS, PISTACHIOS & ORANGE BLOSSOM WATER 221
PECAN, PARSNIP, APPLE & MAPLE SYRUP CAKE 222
PEAR, ALMOND & CHOCOLATE CAKE 224
DATE, OAT & CINNAMON COOKIES 227
ODETTE'S COCONUT ROUGHS 228
ALMOND & PISTACHIO BISCOTTI 230
AMBER'S CHOCOLATE BROWNIE BISCUITS 233
MINI ECLAIRS WITH CHOCOLATE CREAM & PEANUT & CASHEW BRITTLE 235
PEANUT & CASHEW BRITTLE WITH SICHUAN PEPPER & CHILLI 236
MERINGUE 238
TROPICANA ROCKY ROAD 241
RASPBERRY SHERBET MARSHMALLOWS 243

CARROT, PINEAPPLE & WALNUT MUFFINS WITH CREAM CHEESE ICING

Pineapple makes a fresh and zippy surprise in these super-moist carrot muffins.

Preheat the oven to 175°C fan-forced (195°C conventional). Line a large muffin tray with eight paper liners.

Mix the flour, baking powder, bicarbonate of soda, cinnamon, cloves, salt and sugar in a large bowl until combined. Mix in the eggs and oil until combined. Add the carrot, pineapple, walnuts, orange juice and half the zest and mix until just combined.

Divide the mix evenly between the paper liners and bake for 20–25 minutes. Cool completely on a wire rack before icing.

To make the cream cheese icing, mix the cream cheese, icing sugar and lemon juice in a blender.

Spread the icing on each muffin and sprinkle over the extra walnuts and remaining orange zest.

MAKES 8 LARGE MUFFINS

220 g plain flour
1 teaspoon baking powder
1 teaspoon bicarbonate of soda
1 teaspoon ground cinnamon
½ teaspoon ground cloves
½ teaspoon salt flakes
175 g brown sugar
2 extra-large eggs, lightly beaten
90 ml mild olive oil
400 g grated carrot
300 g fresh pineapple, finely diced and gently squeezed of juice (discard the juice)
80 g walnuts, chopped, plus extra to garnish
finely grated zest of 1 orange and juice of ½ orange

CREAM CHEESE ICING
250 g cream cheese, at room temperature
150 g pure icing sugar, sifted
juice of ½ lemon

RED VELVET CUPCAKES WITH MARSHMALLOW ICING

For all the red velvet cupcake fans out there, this recipe is a must-try. The marshmallow icing is deliciously light and fluffy, and the freeze-dried raspberry powder gives these party treats a really tasty zing.

Preheat the oven to 175°C fan-forced (195°C conventional). Line a medium cupcake tray with 18 paper liners.

To make the cupcakes, place the butter, sugar, eggs, flour, cocoa powder, baking powder and vanilla in the bowl of a food processor and process until smooth. Gradually add the milk and red colouring, while processing, until the mixture is smooth and evenly combined.

Spoon the mixture into the liners until they're two-thirds full. Bake for 15–20 minutes until springy to the touch. Cool on wire racks.

To make the marshmallow icing, add the egg whites to the bowl of an electric mixer with the whisk attachment fitted. Don't beat yet. Heat the sugar and 100 ml of water in a medium saucepan over high heat. Using a sugar thermometer to monitor the temperature, bring the syrup up to 115°C. As soon as the syrup has come to temperature, whisk the egg whites on high speed until soft peaks form.

When the temperature reaches 121°C, pour the syrup in a slow continuous stream into the egg whites while whisking. This will cook the egg whites and increase the volume threefold. Keep whisking the meringue for 5 minutes until cool.

Spoon the meringue into a piping bag with a large nozzle attached and decorate the cooled cupcakes – you could also simply spoon the icing on. Sprinkle over some freeze-dried raspberry powder or shaved chocolate (if using).

MAKES 18

250 g unsalted butter, softened
200 g caster sugar
4 extra-large eggs
240 g self-raising flour
35 g cocoa powder
2 teaspoons baking powder
2 teaspoons vanilla extract
120 ml milk
2 tablespoons red food colouring
freeze-dried raspberry powder, to serve
shaved chocolate, to serve (optional)

MARSHMALLOW ICING
100 g egg whites (approximately 3 extra-large egg whites but accuracy is important)
220 g caster sugar

STICKY SEMOLINA CAKE WITH ALMONDS, PISTACHIOS & ORANGE BLOSSOM WATER

The fragrant little morsels of this cake remind me of childhood visits to various aunts and uncles on dad's side of the family. There'd always be something small, sticky and sweet on offer, and you were never allowed to have just one. Perfect with good black coffee or tea.

Preheat the oven to 170°C fan-forced (190°C conventional). Butter a 30 cm × 30 cm baking tray – you can also use a round or rectangular tray, but just make sure it has a 3–5-cm lip to take the mix and syrup.

Mix the semolina, sugar, yoghurt, coconut, almond meal, flour, milk, butter and vanilla in a large bowl until well combined.

Spread the mix onto the prepared tray, pushing it flat with a spatula. Cut into a diamond pattern and dot each diamond with a pistachio and an almond – you can make the diamonds any size you like, you'll just require more, or less, nuts to garnish. Bake for 35 minutes until golden.

To make the orange blossom syrup, boil the sugar and 200 ml of water in a saucepan for 3 minutes. Turn off the heat and stir through the lemon juice and orange blossom water. Set aside to cool.

Once the cake is cooked, remove from the oven and immediately pour the syrup evenly over the top. Set aside to cool and take up the syrup.

You can eat the semolina cake warm after about 20 minutes, or cool completely. It will keep for around 4 days covered in plastic wrap.

MAKES 30 PIECES

450 g fine semolina
220 g caster sugar
200 g thick plain yoghurt
50 g desiccated coconut
50 g almond meal
75 g self-raising flour
3 tablespoons milk
200 g unsalted butter, melted
1 teaspoon vanilla extract
30 unsalted shelled pistachios
30 blanched almonds

ORANGE BLOSSOM SYRUP
300 g caster sugar
1 tablespoon lemon juice
2 tablespoons orange blossom water

PECAN, PARSNIP, APPLE & MAPLE SYRUP CAKE

Olive oil and apple give this cake such an incredibly moist texture.

Preheat the oven to 160°C fan-forced (180°C conventional). Butter a 26-cm round cake tin.

To make the cake, dry whisk the flour, sugar, baking powder, bicarbonate of soda, spices and salt in a large bowl.

In another bowl, whisk the eggs, oil and maple syrup until combined.

Add the egg mix to the dry ingredients and mix well. Fold in the parsnip, apple and pecans and pour into the prepared tin. Bake for 30 minutes.

Just before the 30 minutes are up, prepare the maple glaze. Add all the ingredients to a small saucepan over medium heat and stir until incorporated.

Slide the oven rack out a little and pour the glaze over the cake. Bake for a further 50–60 minutes, or until a skewer inserted in the centre comes out clean. Remove from the oven and set aside for around 10 minutes. Run a knife around the edge of the cake and turn out, then transfer to a wire rack to cool completely.

To make the icing, mix all the ingredients in a large bowl until smooth.

Ice the cake once cooled.

SERVES 8–10

375 g plain flour
280 g caster sugar
2 teaspoons baking powder
1½ teaspoons bicarbonate of soda
2 teaspoons ground cinnamon
1 teaspoon freshly grated nutmeg
2 teaspoons ground ginger
2 teaspoons salt flakes
4 extra-large eggs
350 ml mild olive oil
100 ml maple syrup
250 g grated parsnip (approximately 3 parsnips)
1 × 400 g can pie apples
180 g pecans, roughly chopped

MAPLE GLAZE

2 tablespoons light olive oil
100 g maple syrup
2 teaspoons ground ginger
2½ tablespoons milk
60 g pecans

CREAM CHEESE ICING

250 g cream cheese, at room temperature
150 g pure icing sugar, sifted
juice of ½ lemon

PEAR, ALMOND & CHOCOLATE CAKE

This moist, gluten-free cake has a generous helping of fruit and dark chocolate with a deliciously buttery crumb. Enjoy for afternoon tea or warm for dessert with a large dollop of double cream.

Preheat the oven to 160°C fan-forced (180°C conventional). Butter and line a 24-cm springform cake tin.

Combine the almond meal, coconut and sugar in a large bowl.

In another large bowl, whisk the eggs, vanilla, maple syrup and nutmeg until lightly frothy. Whisk in the melted butter, add to the dry mix and combine.

Pour half the batter into the prepared tin, top with half the sliced pear, scatter over half the chocolate, then add the rest of the batter. Top with the remaining pear and chocolate. Tap gently on the bench to settle and bake for 70 minutes. Remove from the oven and cool completely in the tin.

Once cool, unmould the cake and serve slices with a dollop of plain yoghurt and a drizzle of maple syrup.

SERVES 8

340 g almond meal
60 g desiccated coconut
200 g caster sugar
4 extra-large eggs
2 teaspoons vanilla extract
2½ tablespoons maple syrup, plus extra to serve
½ whole nutmeg, finely grated
200 g unsalted butter, melted and cooled at room temperature
3 ripe pears, peeled, cored and each cut in 12 wedges
100 g dark chocolate buttons (70% cocoa)
thick plain yoghurt, to serve

DATE, OAT & CINNAMON COOKIES

Everything I want from a cookie (insert tall glass of milk or strong cup of coffee here).

Add the flour, cinnamon, salt, bicarbonate of soda, caster sugar and brown sugar to a large bowl and dry-whisk until combined.

Whisk the butter with an electric mixer for a few minutes until soft and fluffy. Add the egg and vanilla and whisk until combined. The mixture may separate but it won't affect the outcome. Add the dry mix in two additions and beat until combined. Add the oats and dates and mix on low to combine. Refrigerate the mix for 30 minutes.

Preheat the oven to 170°C fan-forced (190°C conventional). Line two baking trays with baking paper.

Evenly divide the chilled dough into 14–16 portions, roll into balls and generously space out on the prepared trays. Flatten a little and set aside for 10 minutes before baking for 12–15 minutes until golden. Set aside to cool.

MAKES 14–16 COOKIES

150 g plain flour
2 teaspoons ground cinnamon
1 teaspoon salt flakes
2 teaspoons bicarbonate of soda
60 g caster sugar
140 g brown sugar
160 g unsalted butter, softened
1 extra-large egg
2 teaspoons vanilla extract
150 g rolled oats
150 g pitted dates, chopped

ODETTE'S COCONUT ROUGHS

My sister, Odette, is a pastry chef and she was kind enough to give me this great little recipe. Chewy, buttery deliciousness.

Preheat the oven to 160°C fan-forced (180°C conventional). Line a baking tray with baking paper.

Add half the rolled oats and shaved coconut to the bowl of a food processor and blitz to a crumb-like consistency. Tip into a large bowl.

Add the flour, sugar, nutmeg and remaining coconut and oats to the bowl and combine.

Add the butter, golden syrup and 3½ tablespoons of water to a small saucepan and bring to the boil. Stir the bicarbonate of soda into the boiling liquid and immediately pour over the dry ingredients. Mix until well combined.

Evenly divide into 12 portions, roll into balls, place on the prepared tray and flatten slightly. The biscuits will spread to around double their diameter once baked, so leave enough space between each. Lightly sprinkle with salt and bake for 15 minutes until golden.

MAKES 12 BISCUITS

60 g rolled oats
170 g shaved coconut, plus extra to garnish
150 g plain flour
200 g caster sugar
½ whole nutmeg, finely grated
100 g unsalted butter
30 g golden syrup
5 g bicarbonate of soda
salt flakes

ALMOND & PISTACHIO BISCOTTI

These pretty little biscuits are the perfect after-dinner treat with coffee or tea.

Add the blanched almonds, 270 g of caster sugar and 3 egg whites to the bowl of a food processor and process until smooth. Add the mix to a large bowl.

Add the remaining caster sugar and egg white, the hazelnuts, almond meal, butter and honey to the food processor and process until well combined. Add to the bowl with the almond mixture and combine. Cover with plastic wrap and refrigerate for 1 hour.

Preheat the oven to 140°C fan-forced (160°C conventional). Line two baking trays with baking paper.

Combine the pine nuts and pistachios in a shallow bowl.

Roll the chilled biscotti mix into walnut-sized balls (approximately 25 g each). Roll each ball in the chopped pistachios and pine nuts and stud with the extra pistachios, a glacé cherry or almond, or roll in icing sugar. Place on the prepared trays, flatten out slightly and bake for 20 minutes until pale golden. Remove from the oven and set aside to cool.

The biscotti will keep in an airtight container for up to 4 days.

MAKES APPROXIMATELY 50 BISCOTTI

- 120 g blanched almonds
- 570 g caster sugar
- 4 extra-large egg whites, keep one white separate from the other three
- 100 g hazelnuts, toasted and skins rubbed off
- 300 g almond meal
- 80 g unsalted butter, softened
- 1 tablespoon honey
- 150 g pine nuts, roughly chopped
- 200 g unsalted shelled pistachios, roughly chopped, plus extra to garnish
- glacé cherries, to garnish
- blanched almonds, to garnish
- pure icing sugar, for dusting

AMBER'S CHOCOLATE BROWNIE BISCUITS

These biscuits are rich and decadent with a velvety texture. I love them, but one's enough for me. My daughter, Amber, can eat two. They're her favourite.

Melt half of the chocolate and the butter in a large stainless steel bowl over a saucepan with a few centimetres of barely simmering water in it. Once the chocolate is about two-thirds melted, take the bowl off the saucepan and stir through briefly until combined. Set aside to cool.

Using an electric mixer with the whisk attached, beat the eggs, vanilla, sugar and cocoa powder for about 5 minutes until thick and creamy. Pour the cooled chocolate into the mixing bowl and fold in until combined. Add the flour and almond meal and fold through, then fold through the remaining chopped chocolate.

Lay out two lengths of foil with a sheet of baking paper on top of each. Divide the mix in two and place half on each sheet of baking paper. Form each portion into a log about 6-cm thick and roll up, shaping into even rolls as you do. Twist the ends to seal. Place in the fridge for 1 hour. If the dough has been left in the fridge for a bit longer it will need to be brought back to room temperature before baking.

When you're ready to bake, preheat the oven to 160°C fan-forced (180°C conventional). Line two baking trays with baking paper.

Unroll the chilled dough and cut with a sharp knife into 2-cm thick discs. Roll into balls and place on the prepared trays. Leave a few centimetres between each, as they will spread. Flatten each ball a little and bake for 8–10 minutes. They will be quite soft straight from the oven so let them cool fully on the tray before serving.

MAKES APPROXIMATELY 30

500 g dark chocolate (70% cocoa), roughly chopped
45 g unsalted butter
3 extra-large eggs
½ teaspoon vanilla extract
200 g caster sugar
2 tablespoons cocoa powder
120 g plain flour
150 g almond meal

MINI ECLAIRS WITH CHOCOLATE CREAM & PEANUT & CASHEW BRITTLE

This is not a recipe for the time-poor. There's more than a little work involved, but for the keen pastry cook these eclairs are the perfect project for a special event. The choux pastry is a great recipe and you can make profiteroles or larger eclairs if you like. You could also fill them with whipped cream and drizzle with melted chocolate for a tasty shortcut.

To make the choux pastry, bring the water, butter and salt to a simmer in a small saucepan over medium heat. Remove from the heat. Tip the flour and sugar into the pan and stir with a wooden spoon until combined. Return to the heat for 1–2 minutes while stirring constantly. The mix will form into one mass and start to pull away from the sides of the pan. Remove from the heat once the dough is glossy and smooth. Immediately transfer the dough to the bowl of an electric mixer with a K-beater attached. Mix on slow for 30 seconds. Add a third of the egg and continue mixing on slow until incorporated. Repeat in two more additions, making sure the egg is incorporated before making the next addition. Increase to medium speed and mix for 20 seconds. The dough should be able to hold a peak but then slowly flop down over itself.

Spoon the choux pastry into a piping bag with a plain or star nozzle and chill in the fridge for 1 hour – the choux can be chilled for longer and overnight if necessary.

Preheat the oven to 200°C fan-forced. Line two baking trays with baking paper.

Pipe 6–8-cm lines of choux onto the prepared trays, leaving 5 cm between each line. Wet your fingers (or use an atomiser) and flick water over the trays – the steam generated in the oven will help the choux rise – and place the trays in the oven. Immediately reduce the oven to 180°C and bake for 30 minutes, or until the eclairs are puffed and golden. Turn the trays around in the oven, reduce the heat to 160°C and bake for a further 10 minutes. Set aside to cool.

Melt the chocolate in a large stainless steel bowl over a medium saucepan with a few centimetres of barely simmering water in it. Remove the bowl from the pan.

Using a mortar and pestle, smash the brittle into a chunky powder.

Slice the cooled eclairs open. Pipe the chocolate pastry cream along the length of each, dust with the smashed brittle, top with the other half and drizzle over some melted chocolate.

MAKES 25–35

CHOUX PASTRY
240 g water
120 g unsalted butter
2 g salt
175 g plain flour
35 g caster sugar
250 g eggs (approximately 4–5 extra-large eggs but accuracy is essential)

TO SERVE
150 g dark chocolate (70% cocoa), chopped
½ quantity Peanut & Cashew Brittle (see page 236)
½ quantity Chocolate Pastry Cream (see page 194)

PEANUT & CASHEW BRITTLE WITH SICHUAN PEPPER & CHILLI

This is a bit of an adult confection with a good lick of salt and creeping chilli heat. Eat as is, or crush to a chunky powder and sprinkle over ice cream and other desserts. For an extra-indulgent treat, try my Mini Eclairs (see page 235).

Preheat the oven to 180°C fan-forced (200°C conventional). Line a baking tray with baking paper.

Lightly whisk the egg white in a large bowl until foaming. Mix in the salt, chilli and Sichuan pepper. Add the cashews and peanuts and mix to thoroughly coat the nuts. Spread in a thin layer on the prepared tray and roast for 5 minutes, mix through and roast for 2 more minutes. Remove from the oven and set aside to cool for 10 minutes.

Using a mortar and pestle, crush a large handful of the nuts to a rough powder.

Add the crushed nuts, whole nuts and baking soda to a large bowl and mix. Add the softened butter and set aside.

Line a baking tray with baking paper.

Bring the sugar, honey and 100 ml of water to a simmer in a medium saucepan. Cook until the caramel reaches 145°C on a sugar thermometer. Tip in the nut mix, stirring until the foaming subsides and the butter is completely incorporated. Immediately pour the mix onto the prepared tray and, working quickly, spread flat with a spatula. Lay a piece of baking paper on top of the brittle and press down with a second tray until as flat as possible. Set aside to cool completely before breaking into pieces. Store in an airtight container.

MAKES ABOUT 800 G

1 egg white
½ teaspoon salt flakes
1 teaspoon dried chilli flakes, ground
1 teaspoon finely crushed Sichuan peppercorns
150 g salted cashews
250 g salted peanuts
⅓ teaspoon baking soda
30 g unsalted butter, softened
265 g caster sugar
120 g honey

MERINGUE

Use this recipe whenever you need meringue. Pipe or spoon into any shape you like and sprinkle with freeze-dried raspberry or passionfruit powder for sweet little treats. Crush or smash pieces for a classic Eton mess or my take on it (see page 211), or serve with curd and fresh fruit for a deconstructed pavlova.

Preheat the oven to 120°C conventional. Line a baking tray with baking paper.

Beat the egg whites in the bowl of an electric mixer – making sure the bowl is clean and completely dry – until soft peaks form. Incorporate the icing sugar in three batches while beating. Keep beating until the mix is glossy and stiff enough to hold its shape – you can test this by spooning some meringue back onto the mass; if it holds its form, it's ready.

Off the mixer, gently fold in the cornflour, cream of tartar and vinegar until incorporated.

Spoon 2 teaspoons of the mix into an oblong on the prepared tray to make each meringue. Bake for 90 minutes. Turn the oven off and open the door a fraction. Leave to cool completely in the oven.

MAKES 8–10 MERINGUES

160 ml egg whites (approximately 4 extra-large whites but accuracy is essential), make sure there are no traces of yolk
280 g pure icing sugar, sifted
3 tablespoons cornflour
1 teaspoon cream of tartar
2½ teaspoons white vinegar

TROPICANA ROCKY ROAD

This white chocolate version of rocky road has a bit of a tropical theme. Cut into pieces and keep in an airtight container, or wrap in cellophane tied with ribbon to make festive gifts.

Spray and line a brownie tray – you could also use a lamington tin or muffin tray or fill rings on baking paper.

Spread out the finely chopped chocolate evenly (rather than in a mound) in a large stainless steel bowl and place over a medium saucepan with a few centimetres of barely simmering water in it. When about two-thirds of the chocolate has melted, stir through once. Add the coconut oil and stir a couple more times to ensure that all the chocolate melts – don't mix too much, or overheat, as the chocolate will become grainy. Take the bowl off the pan.

Combine the remaining ingredients, except for the passionfruit powder and a few cherries and marshmallows reserved for garnish, in a large bowl. Pour in the melted chocolate and fold through. Stand for 2 minutes, then pour onto the prepared tray. Decorate with the reserved cherries, marshmallows and extra coconut and sprinkle over the passionfruit powder. Allow a couple of hours at room temperature to properly set – you could speed this up by popping it in the fridge for 30 minutes, but don't leave it any longer.

Lift out of the tin and slice into pieces. Store in an airtight container somewhere cool.

MAKES APPROXIMATELY 1 KG

450 g white chocolate, 400 g finely chopped and 50 g in chunks
100 ml coconut oil (if in a solid state, warm gently to melt)
140 g white marshmallows, cut in half
100 g shaved coconut, plus extra to garnish
80 g candied papaya, roughly diced
150 g lemon Turkish delight (or any kind you like), cut into 3-cm × 1-cm pieces
90 g red glacé cherries
120 g glacé pineapple, roughly diced
180 g salted toasted macadamia nuts
3 tablespoons dried passionfruit powder

RASPBERRY SHERBET MARSHMALLOWS

These marshmallows have such a lovely raspberry flavour and the natural sharpness of the fruit balances against the sugar. The dusting sugar adds a sherbetty fizz that takes me straight back to childhood. They also add a special touch to my Martini Mess (see page 211).

Soak the gelatine leaves in cold water for 5 minutes.

Lightly oil and line a 23-cm square cake tin.

Add the raspberry juice to a medium bowl. Squeeze any excess water from the gelatine before adding it to the raspberry juice.

Add the caster sugar and 150 ml of water to a medium saucepan and stir over low heat until the sugar has dissolved. Increase the heat to medium and cook for a further 5–10 minutes until the syrup reaches 125°C on a sugar thermometer. Remove from the heat, add the raspberry juice and stir to dissolve the gelatine.

Beat the egg whites and a pinch of salt in an electric mixer until soft peaks form. Gradually add the hot raspberry mixture in a steady stream while beating on medium speed. The mixture will double in size and become thick and glossy. Continue beating for 6 minutes until cooled.

Pour the marshmallow mix into the prepared tin and flatten out with a spatula. Set aside at room temperature for 3–4 hours until firm.

For the dusting sugar, combine the icing sugar, cornflour and citric acid in a small bowl.

Turn the marshmallow out onto a board or clean bench and cut into cubes with a sharp knife. Roll in the dusting sugar and use. You can store the marshmallows in an airtight container for up to a week, just roll in the dusting sugar before using. Don't refrigerate.

MAKES APPROXIMATELY 30 PIECES

10 gold-strength gelatine leaves
300 g frozen raspberries, thawed, blitzed, strained and gently warmed
550 g caster sugar
100 g egg whites (approximately 3 extra-large whites but accuracy is essential) at room temperature
pinch of salt

DUSTING SUGAR
5 tablespoons pure icing sugar
3 tablespoons cornflour
1 tablespoon citric acid

CHRISTMAS

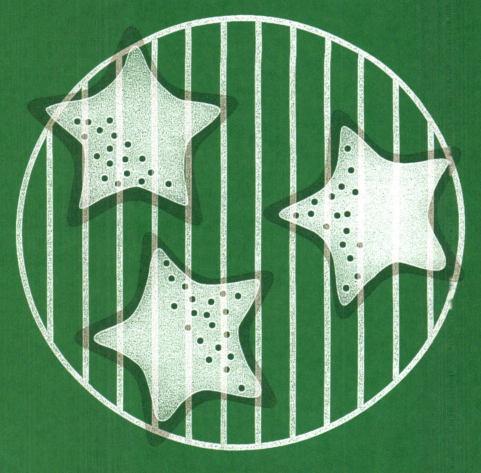

CRISPY PRAWN, CRAB & SHIITAKE CIGAR ROLLS 246

JAMON WITH ROCKMELON, MINT & SHERRY VINEGAR JELLY 248

CHICKEN LIVER PARFAIT WITH ITALIAN FLAVOURS 252

CITRUS-CURED OCEAN TROUT GRAVLAX 255

RUSSIAN SALAD WITH PRAWNS, CRAB & SALMON CAVIAR 256

CHRISTMAS CHICKEN 259

SPICED PORK FILLET WITH ROASTED CHERRY & APPLE CHUTNEY 260

PORCHETTA WITH RYE, APPLE, PRUNE & SAGE STUFFING 264

PAVLOVA WITH PINEAPPLE, PINK PEPPERCORNS & CITRUS CURD 266

STRAWBERRY TRIFLE 269

STELLA'S GINGERBREAD STAR COOKIES 270

CRISPY PRAWN, CRAB & SHIITAKE CIGAR ROLLS

These are my absolute favourite spring rolls. Wrap them in iceberg with plenty of herbs for a fresh and crisp contrast to the crunchy, golden rolls.

Add the prawns to the bowl of a food processor and blitz for 20 seconds.

Combine the blitzed prawns, soy sauce, fish sauce, sesame oil, sugar, pepper, shiitake, spring onion and garlic in a large bowl. Add the crabmeat and mix well.

Lay a spring roll wrapper on a clean work surface. Brush three edges with the egg wash, place 1 tablespoon of filling along the fourth edge and roll up tightly. Press the ends together to seal and fray the edges with a knife for presentation. Repeat with the remaining wrappers and filling.

Preheat the deep fryer or about 8 cm of oil in a large, wide-based saucepan to 180°C.

Working in batches, fry the rolls for 2–3 minutes until golden brown, turning halfway through cooking. Drain briefly on paper towel and serve immediately.

Serve the cigar rolls with the nuoc cham, lettuce and herbs on the side.

MAKES 25 ROLLS

500 g green prawn cutlets, peeled and deveined
1 tablespoon soy sauce
2 tablespoons fish sauce
1 teaspoon sesame oil
½ teaspoon caster sugar
½ teaspoon freshly ground black pepper
5 shiitake mushrooms, stems discarded and caps diced
6 spring onions, finely sliced
2 garlic cloves, finely grated
200 g cooked crabmeat, drained
1 packet of large spring roll wrappers
1 egg, lightly beaten with 1 tablespoon water
vegetable oil, for deep frying
1 quantity Nuoc Cham (see page 94)
1 crisp iceberg lettuce
½ bunch of Thai basil
½ bunch of Vietnamese mint

JAMON WITH ROCKMELON, MINT & SHERRY VINEGAR JELLY

This is such an old-school combination. The sherry vinegar and verjuice jelly acts like a dressing, giving little pops of contrast to the sweet melon and rich and salty jamon.

Soak the gelatine sheets in cold water for 5 minutes.

Add the vinegar and verjuice to a small saucepan, bring just up to a simmer and take off the heat.

Gently squeeze the gelatine of excess water and add to the pan. Stir until the gelatine has dissolved and pour into a small plastic container to set – this will take a couple of hours.

Cut the ends off the rockmelon and peel. Scoop out the seeds and slice into 3-mm thick discs. Twist the discs and arrange on a serving plate with the slices of jamon. Scrape off rough strips of jelly with a spoon and dot over the plate, season with a little salt and pepper, scatter over the mint leaves, drizzle with oil and serve.

SERVES 4

4 gold-strength gelatine sheets
100 ml sherry vinegar
100 ml verjuice
1 small rockmelon
12 slices of jamon (or prosciutto)
salt flakes and freshly ground black pepper
1 handful of mint leaves
extra virgin olive oil

CHICKEN LIVER PARFAIT WITH ITALIAN FLAVOURS

This parfait has such a lusciously smooth texture with hints of citrus and spice. Serve with your favourite pickles, shaved mustard fruit or sweet onion jam. I also love to contrast the silky richness with bitter radicchio leaves.

Add the livers and milk to a bowl, cover and refrigerate overnight. Drain the livers, dry well on paper towel and trim off any connective tissue.

Set the diced butter aside at room temperature. Melt the remaining butter in a small saucepan with the bay leaves and thyme. Set aside to infuse.

Sweat the shallots and garlic in a medium saucepan with a little oil until softened. Add the Montenegro and reduce to a glaze.

Mix the white pepper, nutmeg, cinnamon and allspice together in a small bowl.

Heat a large frying pan over high heat until hot. Lightly oil the livers and sear quickly in three batches, seasoning well with salt as you go. Flip the livers after 1 minute and add a third of the diced butter and a third of the spice mix. Once the other side is seared, deglaze with a third of the brandy and immediately lift the livers out of the pan – the livers should still be rare. Boil the brandy for 20 seconds and pour into a separate container. Wipe out the pan and repeat.

Remove the herbs from the melted butter.

In a blender, puree the livers with the reserved liquid in two batches, adding the cream and melted butter as you go. Mix the batches together, check for seasoning and pass through a very fine sieve. Pour the parfait mix into dishes or jars and set in the fridge. Use within 5 days.

Serve the parfait with cornichons and toasted baguette or crostini.

MAKES 1 LARGE OR 4–6 SMALL POTS

800 g chicken livers (it is essential that these are really fresh)
800 ml milk
300 g butter, half diced
2 fresh bay leaves
6 thyme sprigs
5 French shallots, finely diced
4 garlic cloves, chopped
extra virgin olive oil
250 ml Amaro Montenegro (an Italian digestive liqueur)
1 teaspoon freshly ground white pepper
½ whole nutmeg, finely grated
½ teaspoon ground cinnamon
½ teaspoon ground allspice
salt flakes
250 ml brandy
120 ml cream
cornichons, to serve
toasted baguette or crostini, to serve

CITRUS-CURED OCEAN TROUT GRAVLAX

Gravlax is a favourite in my house all year round, but I always cure a side of ocean trout for Christmas, and it's inevitably the first platter I have to replenish. When choosing a piece of ocean trout to cure, take a piece from the head end rather than the tail. The more even the thickness of the fillet, the more consistent the result.

Mix the salt, sugar, citrus juice and zest in a medium bowl until you have an even slurry.

In a ceramic dish or deep tray that will fit the trout lying flat, lay in two lengths of plastic wrap so that they overhang each end of the dish and overlap each other. Press the lengths together along the join. Spoon about a third of the slurry along the length of the dish and place the trout, skin-side down, on top. Spoon the rest of the slurry over the flesh. Pull the edges of plastic wrap together tightly, pushing the cure evenly over the fish, and seal. Refrigerate for 8 hours, opening the parcel and turning the fish once after 4 hours.

Once cured, lift the fish out of the slurry and wipe clean with damp paper towel – don't wash the cure off. Brush the flesh with a fine layer of mustard and evenly press on the chopped dill. Wrap tightly in plastic wrap and press the flesh side of the wrapped trout against your benchtop to help the dill to stick. Ideally refrigerate for another hour before serving.

Serve the thinly sliced gravlax with rye or white toast, chopped onion, grated hard-boiled egg, watercress, caperberries, cornichons, crème fraîche, a squeeze of lemon or anything else that takes your fancy.

SERVES 15–20

200 g rock salt
100 g caster sugar
finely grated zest and juice of 1 lemon
finely grated zest and juice of 1 orange
1 × 1.2–1.5 kg side of ocean trout (or salmon), pin-boned, skin on
1½ tablespoons Dijon mustard
1 bunch of dill, fronds picked and chopped

TO SERVE
rye or white toast
chopped red onion
grated hard-boiled eggs
watercress, picked
caperberries
cornichons
crème fraîche
lemon wedges

RUSSIAN SALAD WITH PRAWNS, CRAB & SALMON CAVIAR

Christmas at my house just isn't complete without a Russian salad. It's never the same year to year, but it's always full of beautifully fresh seafood with herbs, hard-boiled eggs and homemade mayonnaise.

Boil the potato in salted water until tender. Drain well.

Boil the carrot in salted water until tender. Drain well.

Add the warm potato and carrot to a large bowl with the vinegar and 2 tablespoons of oil, season with salt and pepper and toss gently. Set aside for 5–10 minutes to take up the flavour and cool a little.

Combine the mayonnaise and crème fraîche in a small bowl and add to the cooled potato and carrot. Gently toss to combine and pile onto a serving platter. Top with the slices of egg and scatter the crabmeat around the edges.

Add the prawns, spring onion, chilli, chives and dill to a large bowl, drizzle with oil, season with salt and pepper, squeeze over lemon juice to taste and combine. Pile the prawns into the middle of the salad, spoon over the salmon caviar and serve.

SERVES 8

4 Dutch cream potatoes, peeled and cut into 2-cm discs
3 carrots, peeled and cut into 1.5-cm dice
2 tablespoons white wine vinegar
extra virgin olive oil
salt flakes and freshly ground black pepper
3 tablespoons quality mayonnaise
3 tablespoons crème fraîche (or thick plain yoghurt)
2 hard-boiled eggs, thinly sliced but try to keep the slices intact
150 g cooked crabmeat
12 cooked prawns, peeled and deveined
2 spring onions, finely sliced
1 long green chilli, finely sliced
½ bunch of chives, snipped into 3-cm batons
1 handful of dill fronds
1 lemon
2 tablespoons salmon caviar

CHRISTMAS CHICKEN

This spicy stuffing with plenty of dried fruit and nuts makes for such a festive bird. The pancetta protects and bastes the breast as it cooks, while the potatoes take up all of the beautiful cooking juices.

Preheat the oven to 180°C fan-forced (200°C conventional).

For the stuffing, place the dried fruit and vinegar in a small saucepan and simmer for 2 minutes. Remove from the heat and set aside for 20 minutes. Heat the oil in a frying pan over medium heat. Add the onion and garlic, reduce the heat and cook for 10–15 minutes until sticky and caramelised. Add the ground cloves, nutmeg and half the butter (not the diced and chilled portion). Stir until the butter has melted, add the thyme and bring the butter to a sizzle. Add the pistachios and soaked fruit and vinegar, season with salt and pepper and take off the heat. Tip the mixture into a large bowl and mix through the breadcrumbs, parsley and cheese. Add the diced chilled butter and mix until combined.

Season the cavity of the chicken with salt and pepper and fill with the stuffing. Truss the legs together and place in a large roasting dish. Rub the chicken with a little oil and season. Scatter the potatoes around the chicken, season and drizzle with a little oil. Lay the pancetta slices evenly over the breast and roast for 75–90 minutes until golden and cooked. If the pancetta is browning too much, cover the breast loosely with a piece of foil, allowing the legs to continue to brown. Rest for 10–20 minutes before carving.

SERVES 4–6

---

1 × 1.6–1.8 kg chicken
salt flakes and freshly ground black pepper
extra virgin olive oil
6 large desiree potatoes, peeled and quartered
16 long slices of flat pancetta

STUFFING

125 g dried cherries, cranberries and currants (or just use one or two of these)
100 ml red wine vinegar
2 tablespoons extra virgin olive oil
1 large brown onion, finely diced
5 garlic cloves, finely sliced
1 teaspoon ground cloves
¼ whole nutmeg, finely grated
80 g butter, 40 g diced and chilled
5 thyme sprigs, leaves picked
100 g pistachios, roughly chopped
salt flakes and freshly ground black pepper
1½ cups fresh breadcrumbs
2 handfuls of flat-leaf parsley leaves, chopped
30 g Grana Padano cheese, finely grated

SPICED PORK FILLET WITH ROASTED CHERRY & APPLE CHUTNEY

This chutney is somewhere between a regular chutney and a warm salad. It sauces the pork with sweet, sour and spicy juices but also has a really chunky textural quality. The trick is to roast the fruit in a shallow layer so that it doesn't stew.

Preheat the oven to 180°C fan-forced (200°C conventional).

Add all of the chutney ingredients to a large baking dish, season generously with salt and pepper and toss gently to combine. Roast for 30–40 minutes, stirring through a couple of times, until the fruit and onions have softened and the cherries have let out some juice. Set aside in a warm place.

When the chutney is almost ready, heat the barbecue or a large frying pan over medium–high heat. Coat the pork with oil, season with salt and pepper, rub on the Chinese five spice and cook for 4 minutes on each of the three sides of the fillets (12 minutes in total) until just cooked. Rest for 5 minutes before slicing into thick medallions.

Arrange the pork on a serving platter, spoon over the chutney with all the juices and serve.

SERVES 6

2 × 350–400 g pork fillets
olive oil
salt flakes and freshly ground black pepper
1 tablespoon Chinese five spice

ROASTED CHERRY & APPLE CHUTNEY

3 granny smith apples, peeled, cored and cut into rough 2-cm dice
500 g cherries, half whole with stalks attached and the rest halved and pitted
3 small red onions, each sliced into 8 wedges, roots intact (this will help them keep their shape)
3 garlic cloves, smashed, skin on
5-cm piece of ginger, finely julienned
1 cinnamon stick
3 star anise
30 g butter
2 tablespoons extra virgin olive oil
100 ml red wine vinegar
3 tablespoons brown sugar
salt flakes and freshly ground black pepper

PORCHETTA WITH RYE, APPLE, PRUNE & SAGE STUFFING

This is also delicious served cold with a simple bitter leaf salad for Boxing Day lunch. Or stuff slices into a baguette with some provolone or cheddar and a good smear of chutney.

For the stuffing, cover the prunes with boiling water and set aside for 30 minutes. Drain and chop in half. Grill or toast the bread until quite dark, rub all over with the garlic and tear into pieces. Heat a large, deep-sided frying pan over medium heat. Add a good splash of oil and heat until quite hot, but not smoking. Add the sage leaves, season and fry until crisp. Add the apple and toss over high heat until starting to brown. Add the verjuice and simmer for a few minutes until the apple is just tender. Add the prunes, vinegar and a splash of oil to a large bowl and mix. Add the mascarpone and combine. Add the pieces of toasted bread to the apple mix and massage everything well into the dressing.

Preheat the oven to 190°C fan-forced (210°C conventional).

Score the pork skin with a sharp knife. Open the pork out and slash the belly flesh to take up the flavour of the stuffing. Season the flesh generously with salt and pepper and smear with the mustard. Pack in the stuffing next to the loin, roll up tightly and secure firmly with butcher's string in 3-cm sections.

Place the carrots and bay leaves in a large roasting tin, season and drizzle with oil.

Rub the pork with oil and salt and lay on top of the carrots. Pour the stock and 400 ml of verjuice into the tin and roast for 30 minutes. Turn the oven down to 150°C and roast for a further 2 hours. Rest for 25 minutes before slicing thickly.

Serve the porchetta with the carrots and pan juices (reduced if you like).

SERVES 8–10

1 × 4 kg boned pork loin with boned belly attached
salt flakes and freshly ground black pepper
2 tablespoons Dijon mustard
12 medium to large carrots, peeled and split in half lengthways
2 branches of fresh bay leaves
extra virgin olive oil
200 ml chicken stock
400 ml verjuice (or white wine)

STUFFING

200 g pitted prunes
200 g crustless rye sourdough
2 garlic cloves
extra virgin olive oil
5 sage sprigs, picked
salt flakes and freshly ground black pepper
3 granny smith apples, peeled, cored and each cut into 8 wedges
100 ml verjuice (or white wine)
4 tablespoons red wine vinegar
4 tablespoons mascarpone

PAVLOVA WITH PINEAPPLE, PINK PEPPERCORNS & CITRUS CURD

Grilling the pineapple with sugar, lime juice and pink peppercorns adds such a delicious caramelised note to this pavlova, and the tangy citrus curd and unsweetened whipped cream balances out the sweetness.

Preheat the oven to 130°C conventional. Line a baking tray with baking paper.

For the meringue, whisk the egg whites in the bowl of an electric mixer – making sure the bowl is clean and completely dry – until soft peaks form. Incorporate the icing sugar in three batches while whisking. Keep whisking until the mix is glossy and stiff enough to hold its shape – you can test this by spooning some meringue back onto the mass; if it holds its form, it's ready. Off the mixer, gently fold in the cornflour, cream of tartar and vinegar until incorporated.

Immediately tip the meringue mix onto the prepared tray in a dinner plate-sized round and lightly smooth into a dome, but don't flatten the top. Bake for 90 minutes. Turn the oven off and open the door a fraction. Leave to cool completely in the oven.

For the citrus curd, add the eggs and sugar to a large bowl and whisk until combined. Add the citrus juice and whisk until combined. Add the gelatine sheets to a jug of cold water and set aside. Tip the egg mix into a saucepan and whisk constantly over medium heat until the mixture thickens. Cook on low heat for 3 minutes, then take off the heat and whisk for another 3 minutes to cool. Squeeze any excess water from the gelatine and add to the pan. Whisk to combine. Tip the mix into a blender along with the zest and half the butter and blend. Add the remaining butter and blend until smooth. Scoop into a piping bag with a small plain nozzle attached and chill for at least 30 minutes.

Preheat the oven grill to high. Line a baking tray with baking paper.

Using a mortar and pestle, roughly grind the peppercorns and sugar. Add the lime juice and combine.

In a large bowl, toss the pineapple in half of the peppercorn syrup, then place on the prepared tray and grill for 8–10 minutes until starting to caramelise. Set aside to cool on the tray.

To assemble, gently crack the top of the meringue to make a crater, spoon on the whipped cream, slot in the pineapple and pipe on the curd. Finely grate over some lemon zest, spoon over the remaining peppercorn syrup and serve.

SERVES 8–10

3½ tablespoons pink peppercorns
200 g brown sugar
juice of 3 limes
1 whole ripe pineapple, peeled, cut into 16 wedges and core trimmed
400 ml cream, whipped
1 lemon, to serve

MERINGUE
240 ml egg whites (approximately 6–8 extra-large whites, but accuracy is essential), make sure there are no traces of yolk
420 g icing sugar, sifted
4½ tablespoons cornflour
1½ teaspoons cream of tartar
1 tablespoon white vinegar

CITRUS CURD
110 g eggs (approximately 2 extra-large eggs)
110 g caster sugar
120 ml lime and lemon juice (approximately 2 lemons and 2 limes)
2 gold-strength gelatine sheets
finely grated zest of ½ lime
finely grated zest of ½ lemon
140 g unsalted butter, softened

STRAWBERRY TRIFLE

Making your own jelly and custard is really so simple and elevates this dessert into something quite special. Use a large glass bowl to show off all the beautiful components.

To make the jelly, bring the berries, sugar, jam and apple juice to a simmer in a small saucepan and cook for 4 minutes. Set aside for 15 minutes to cool. Soak the gelatine sheets in cold water for 5 minutes. Strain the berry mix, gently pushing out all of the juices with the back of a spoon. You should have about 700 ml of liquid. Gently squeeze the excess water from the gelatine before adding it to the strained liquid. Stir to dissolve the gelatine. Line a plastic container or slice tray with plastic wrap and pour in half of the liquid. Pour the rest into a high-sided glass serving bowl. Place both in the fridge for at least 2 hours for the jelly to set.

To make the custard, combine the vanilla seeds, sugar and cornflour in a large bowl. Whisk in the egg yolks until combined. Add the milk, cream and vanilla bean to a large saucepan over medium heat and simmer for 2 minutes. Slowly pour the hot liquid into the egg mixture while whisking constantly. Pour back into the saucepan and whisk constantly over medium heat until smooth and thickened. Once thickened, pour the custard into a large bowl and chill over iced water, continuing to whisk, on and off, until cool.

To assemble, lift the jelly out of the container and dice. Slice most of the strawberries into thick rounds, leaving some whole to garnish. Press a layer of strawberries around the edge of the bowl. Brush the thinned jam onto one side of each slice of Swiss roll and line the base of the serving bowl. Line the sides with more Swiss roll. Splash the sherry over the cake and pour in the cooled custard. Arrange the diced jelly around the outer edges of the bowl, cover and return to the fridge for at least 1 hour or overnight.

When ready to serve, whip the cream with the icing sugar. Fill the centre of the trifle with the cream and top with the remaining strawberries. Scatter over the toasted almonds and finish with a dusting of icing sugar.

SERVES 8–10

500 g strawberries
125 g strawberry jam, warmed with 2½ tablespoons of water to loosen
3 large Swiss rolls, thickly sliced
100 ml sherry (use your favourite, but I prefer a dry one)
200 ml cream
1 tablespoon pure icing sugar, plus extra to dust
40 g flaked almonds, toasted

JELLY

300 g frozen mixed berries
160 g caster sugar
2 tablespoons strawberry jam
500 ml clear apple juice
9 gold-strength gelatine sheets

VANILLA CUSTARD

1 vanilla bean, split and seeds scraped
150 g caster sugar
4 tablespoons cornflour
6 extra-large egg yolks
680 ml full cream milk
450 ml cream

STELLA'S GINGERBREAD STAR COOKIES

One Christmas, Stella really wanted a gingerbread house but construction just wasn't in the time budget. These soft gingery biscuits made both of us pretty happy. Cut into stars, circles, angels or any shape you like. The mix also freezes well.

Cream the butter and sugars in a food processor. Add the eggs and molasses and process until combined. Add the flour, baking powder and spices and process until you have a smooth dough. Rest in the fridge for 30 minutes.

Preheat the oven to 180°C fan-forced (200°C conventional). Line two baking trays with baking paper.

Roll out the dough on a floured surface until about 1-cm thick. Cut out the cookies with a star cookie cutter (or any shape you like) and carefully lift onto the prepared trays. Leave a couple of centimetres between each and bake for 10–12 minutes until lightly golden. Set aside to cool on the trays, as they will still be quite soft when they come out of the oven.

To make the lemon icing, mix the icing sugar and lemon juice in a medium bowl until you have a smooth honey-like consistency. Adjust with more sugar or lemon juice if needed.

Dip the cooled biscuits in the icing or decorate using a squeeze bottle or piping bag. Decorate with some cachous and place on a wire rack to set.

MAKES APPROXIMATELY 30 COOKIES

160 g unsalted butter, softened
140 g caster sugar
180 g brown sugar
3 extra-large eggs
2 tablespoons molasses
550 g plain flour
1½ teaspoons baking powder
2 teaspoons ground cinnamon
3 teaspoons mixed spice
2 tablespoons ground ginger
cachous (edible silver balls), to decorate

LEMON ICING
300 g pure icing sugar, sifted
juice of 1½ lemons

THANK YOU

To my dear family and friends for your kind words, encouragement, patience and never-ending appetites for pretty much anything I dish up. You know who you are.

To Marcus Ellis for your patience, diligence, sense of humour and attention to detail during this entire project – I couldn't do it without you.

To the talented Chantal Faux – thanks for managing, creating and fielding so many of my personal enquiries, not forgetting those from the public. I treasure our friendship and am lucky to have had your keen ear since the very humble beginnings of the KM brand.

To Mary Small and Jane Winning – thanks for your endless enthusiasm. And thanks to the whole team at Pan Macmillan for channelling fresh vision and energy into this book. I have enjoyed every minute of getting to know you and truly appreciate and admire your expertise in the increasingly competitive world of publishing.

Thanks to proofreader Megan Johnston, typesetter Pauline Haas and indexer Jo Rudd for their editorial attention and eye for detail.

Extra love and a super-big hug to Emma Warren Rodriguez, who was always on hand to help at every level. It was a massive coordination job done extremely well, with lots of laughs along the way.

Big love to Judy Webb, who was there to put anything back together on set and behind the scenes, and was so special to my little ones.

And to Marnie Rowe, who was always there to lend a hand for pretty much anything. I cherish your opinion at all times and your artistic eye – you rock!

Thanks to Paris for tying up all the loose ends and basically coordinating this crazy life I lead with a constant smile, no matter what the request.

To Rachel Walton for not only painting my face beautifully but also lending a hand in the sweets department – another very talented lady.

Special thanks to all chefs and help on hand, both on set and behind the scenes: Kylie Lonergan, Sophie Nilsson, Ben Sisley, Emma Christian, Meryl Batlle, Adam Davis and Sushil Rana. This is a massive achievement and I really appreciate your attention to detail.

To my wonderful, knowledgeable suppliers who always go the extra distance to supply the best and the freshest: Gary McBean at Gary's Quality Meats and Organic Butcher Melbourne at Prahran Market (www.organicbutchermelbourne.com); and Sam and John Narduzzo, Mark and the whole team at Pino's Fine Produce (www.pinosfineproduce.com.au).

Thanks to Caroline Velik, another talented lady in my life. Cheers to another successful project and thanks for your fantastic artistic eye and all the life advice and problem solving along the way. Always a pleasure.

To Mr John Laurie and Tom Friml. Love your work – you guys rock and it's been great doing the second book together. I can confidently say we got some great shots. Come on, I'm joking… the whole book is a complete winner and you really have the food jumping off the pages, fresh and spritely and delicious.

Thanks to the very talented Allison Colpoys, for her clever, clean and fresh designs and drawings.

A big thanks to Cathy Baker, Mark Klemens and Shaun Levin at Profile Management.

Michael, honey, thank you. You keep me grounded, focused, inspired and supported, doing all of this rather effortlessly and laughing all the way. Stella and Amber, from the bottom of my heart, you two are my inspiration and my little treasures. This book wouldn't be so special without all of you.

Karen x

INDEX

A

almonds
    Almond & pistachio biscotti 230
    Celeriac, apple & kale slaw with smoked almonds & dehydrated anchovies 79
    Chocolate ripple & amaretti biscuit cake 202
    Pear, almond & chocolate cake 224
    Prosecco jelly with grapes, whipped ricotta & crushed amaretti biscuits 196
Amber's chocolate brownie biscuits 233
anchovies
    Baked eggs with ratatouille, ricotta & white anchovies 26
    Celeriac, apple & kale slaw with smoked almonds & dehydrated anchovies 79
    Seared rump steak with green chilli & anchovy mayonnaise & green olive salad 186
apples
    Apple & cherry turnovers 205
    Cider-braised smoked bacon with apples & prunes 168
    Free-form apple & blueberry tart 206
    Pecan, parsnip, apple & maple syrup cake 222
    Prune & apple stuffing 264
    Roasted cherry & apple chutney 260
Apricot compote, spiced, with orange blossom labna 12
'Arroz campero' with prawns, calamari & mussels 114
artichoke
    Egg & bacon salad with curly endive, Jerusalem artichoke, shallots & cornichons 80
Avgolemono 63
avocado
    Butter lettuce, tomato, avocado, mozzarella & pickled jalapeño salad 86
    Chicken & corn koftas with avocado & coriander 148
    Cold soba noodles with avocado, bean sprouts, soy, ginger & sesame 92
    Corn & cheddar fritters with avocado, coriander & cumin salt 29

B

bacon
    Broccolini with bacon, shallots, garlic & chilli 103
    Cider-braised smoked bacon with apples & prunes 168
    Egg & bacon salad with curly endive, Jerusalem artichoke, shallots & cornichons 80
    Spiced tomato & chilli soup with smoked bacon 64
Baked blue-eye & prawn parcels with potato, fennel & chermoula 141
Balinese chicken satay 153
banana
    Kale, banana & coconut smoothie 17
    Peanut butter & banana ice cream 199
Barbecued flathead sandwich with iceberg, coriander & sumac aioli 135
Barbecued minute steak with Asian mushroom dressing 180
Barley 'risotto' with pine mushrooms & pancetta 112
beans
    Broad beans & peas with jamon & mint 97
beef
    Barbecued minute steak with Asian mushroom dressing 180
    Beef maltagliata with rocket, radicchio & ricotta 176
    Beef rendang 182
    Egg noodles with shredded beef, Thai basil & sesame 179
    Red-wine braised beef cheeks with celeriac & parsnip puree 185
    Roasted eye fillet with potato dauphinoise & baked camembert 191
    Seared eye fillet with beetroot, goat's cheese, brown butter, cinnamon & sage 188
    Seared rump steak with green chilli & anchovy mayonnaise & green olive salad 186
    Vinaigrette potatoes with cornichons, crème fraîche, fried eggs & corned beef 30
beer
    Lamb shanks braised with beer, honey & oregano 173
beetroot
    Beetroot, quinoa & spinach salad with haloumi, sultanas & dill 82
    Roasted beetroot, cinnamon & pomegranate dip 41
    Seared eye fillet with beetroot, goat's cheese, brown butter, cinnamon & sage 188
    Tuna salad with cucumber, tomato, beetroot, radish & olives 91
berries
    Free-form apple & blueberry tart 206
    Lemon semifreddo with blackberries & lemon syrup 200
    Martini mess 211
    Raspberry sherbet marshmallows 243
    Strawberry trifle 269
biscuits
    Almond & pistachio biscotti 230
    Amber's chocolate brownie biscuits 233
    Date, oat & cinnamon cookies 227
    Odette's coconut roughs 228
    Stella's gingerbread star cookies 270
Bois Boudran dressing 150
bread
    Barbecued flathead sandwich with iceberg, coriander & sumac aioli 135
    Focaccia with red onion, rosemary, olives & chilli 44
    Pita bread 42
    Roast chicken with butter, dill & garlic on a sourdough 'mattress' 165
Broad beans & peas with jamon & mint 97
Broccolini with bacon, shallots, garlic & chilli 103
Butter lettuce, tomato, avocado, mozzarella & pickled jalapeño salad 86

C

cabbage
    Prawn baguette with minted cabbage & sumac 53
    Slaw 160
    Vinaigrette potato salad with shredded cabbage, caraway & lemon 76
cakes
    Carrot, pineapple & walnut muffins with cream cheese icing 216
    Chocolate ripple & amaretti biscuit cake 202
    Deluxe macadamia brownie cake 212
    Mini eclairs with chocolate cream & peanut & cashew brittle 235
    Pear, almond & chocolate cake 224
    Pecan, parsnip, apple & maple syrup cake 222
    Red velvet cupcakes with marshmallow icing 218
    Sticky semolina cake with almonds, pistachios & orange blossom water 221
capsicum
    Ratatouille 109
    Shakshuka 23
carrots
    Carrot, pineapple & walnut muffins with cream cheese icing 216

Roasted carrots with raisins, harissa & coriander 104
cauliflower
    Golden baked pasta with cauliflower & cheese 118
    Roasted cauliflower & parsnip with cumin, chilli & parmesan 98
Celeriac & parsnip puree 185
Celeriac, apple & kale slaw with smoked almonds & dehydrated anchovies 79
cheese
    Beef maltagliata with rocket, radicchio & ricotta 176
    Butter lettuce, tomato, avocado, mozzarella & pickled jalapeño salad 86
    Corn & cheddar fritters with avocado, coriander & cumin salt 29
    Cream cheese icing 216
    Filo pie with greens, ricotta & pumpkin seeds 54
    Fluffy goat's cheese & pea shoot omelette 18
    Golden baked pasta with cauliflower & cheese 118
    Roasted eye fillet with potato dauphinoise & baked camembert 191
    Seared eye fillet with beetroot, goat's cheese, brown butter, cinnamon & sage 188
    Whipped ricotta 196
    see also haloumi
Chermoula 141
cherries
    Apple & cherry turnovers 205
    Roasted cherry & apple chutney 260
chicken
    Avgolemono 63
    Baked chicken with spiced rice, cranberries & dill 162
    Balinese chicken satay 153
    Braised chicken with white wine, Swiss brown mushrooms, pancetta & thyme 159
    Chicken & corn koftas with avocado & coriander 148
    Chicken, kale & mushroom pie 156
    Chicken, olive, lentil & radicchio salad 154
    Chicken, prawn & shiitake pot-sticker dumplings 48
    chicken stock 9
    Chicken vermicelli salad with young coconut, Asian herbs & nuoc cham 94
    Christmas chicken 259
    The mr. wolf chicken schnitzel & slaw 160
    Pan-fried poussin with Bois Boudran dressing 150
    Pressed chicken & prune terrine with apple, celery & watercress 37
    Roast chicken with butter, dill & garlic on a sourdough 'mattress' 165
Chicken liver parfait with Italian flavours 252
chilli
    Broccolini with bacon, shallots, garlic & chilli 103
    Butter lettuce, tomato, avocado, mozzarella & pickled jalapeño salad 86
    Focaccia with red onion, rosemary, olives & chilli 44
    Marinated olives with orange, cinnamon & chilli 34
    Pan-fried salmon with zucchini flowers, fried zucchini, chilli & mint 142
    Peanut & cashew brittle with Sichuan pepper & chilli 236
    Roasted cauliflower & parsnip with cumin, chilli & parmesan 98
    Spiced tomato & chilli soup with smoked bacon 64
chocolate
    Amber's chocolate brownie biscuits 233
    Chocolate pastry cream 194
    Chocolate ripple & amaretti biscuit cake 202
    Deluxe macadamia brownie cake 212
    Mini eclairs with chocolate cream & peanut & cashew brittle 235
    Pear, almond & chocolate cake 224
    Tropicana rocky road 241
Christmas chicken 259
Cider-braised smoked bacon with apples & prunes 168
cinnamon
    Date, oat & cinnamon cookies 227
    Marinated olives with orange, cinnamon & chilli 34
    Roasted beetroot, cinnamon & pomegranate dip 41
    Seared eye fillet with beetroot, goat's cheese, brown butter, cinnamon & sage 188
Citrus curd 266
Citrus-cured ocean trout gravlax 255
coconut
    Chicken vermicelli salad with young coconut, Asian herbs & nuoc cham 94
    Coconut–hoisin dipping sauce 50
    Kale, banana & coconut smoothie 17
    Odette's coconut roughs 228
    Roast pumpkin soup with Thai flavours & young coconut 66
Cold soba noodles with avocado, bean sprouts, soy, ginger & sesame 92
cookies *see* biscuits
corn
    Chicken & corn koftas with avocado & coriander 148
    Corn & cheddar fritters with avocado, coriander & cumin salt 29
Cream cheese icing 216
Crispy prawn, crab & shiitake cigar rolls 246
cucumber
    Pan-fried garfish with taramasalata & soused cucumber, dill & mint salad 136
    Yoghurt, cucumber & mint salad 170
curry
    Beef rendang 182
    Curried rice with egg, seared salmon, peas & spring onion 138
    Scrambled curried tofu with spinach & peas 24

D

Date, oat & cinnamon cookies 227
Deluxe macadamia brownie cake 212
desserts
    Apple & cherry turnovers 205
    Chocolate ripple & amaretti biscuit cake 202
    Deluxe macadamia brownie cake 212
    Free-form apple & blueberry tart 206
    Lemon semifreddo with blackberries & lemon syrup 200
    Martini mess 211
    Meringue 238
    Pavlova with pineapple, pink peppercorns & citrus curd 265
    Peanut & cashew brittle with Sichuan pepper & chilli 236
    Peanut butter & banana ice cream 199
    Prosecco jelly with grapes, whipped ricotta & crushed amaretti biscuits 196
    Raspberry sherbet marshmallows 243
    Roasted peach & pear tarts with vanilla & thyme 208
    Strawberry trifle 269
    Toffeed figs with chocolate pastry cream 194
    see also cakes
dips
    Roasted beetroot, cinnamon & pomegranate dip 41
    Spiced spinach, yoghurt & pine nut dip 41
dressings
    Bois Boudran dressing 150
    French vinaigrette 74
    Mustard cream dressing 37

Nuoc cham 94
Sriracha mayonnaise 47
see also sauces
duck
Roast duck, mushroom & coriander rice paper rolls 50
dumplings
Chicken, prawn & shiitake pot-sticker dumplings 48

E

Egg noodles with shredded beef, Thai basil & sesame 179
eggplant
Grilled eggplant with tahini & yoghurt dressing, pomegranate, chilli & mint 100
Ratatouille 109
eggs
Baked eggs with ratatouille, ricotta & white anchovies 26
Curried rice with egg, seared salmon, peas & spring onion 138
Egg & bacon salad with curly endive, Jerusalem artichoke, shallots & cornichons 80
Fluffy goat's cheese & pea shoot omelette 18
Potato chip tortilla with sriracha mayonnaise 47
Shakshuka 23
Vinaigrette potatoes with cornichons, crème fraîche, fried eggs & corned beef 30

F

fennel
Baked blue-eye & prawn parcels with potato, fennel & chermoula 141
Fennel, orange, currant & olive salad 85
Orzo with prawns & fennel 123
figs
Toffeed figs with chocolate pastry cream 194
Filo pie with greens, ricotta & pumpkin seeds 54
Fluffy goat's cheese & pea shoot omelette 18
Focaccia with red onion, rosemary, olives & chilli 44
Free-form apple & blueberry tart 206
French vinaigrette 74

G

garlic
Broccolini with bacon, shallots, garlic & chilli 103
Pan-roasted snapper with garlic & bay 144
Gazpacho rodriguez 58
Ginger–soy dipping sauce 48
Golden baked pasta with cauliflower & cheese 118
Greek lamb shoulder with yoghurt, cucumber & mint 170
Grilled calamari & prawns with tomato, chilli, parsley, mint & moghrabieh 130

H

haloumi
Beetroot, quinoa & spinach salad with haloumi, sultanas & dill 82
Grilled mushrooms with haloumi, currants, tahini & mint 20
Pork & beef meatloaf with haloumi, pistachios and pomegranate molasses 174
Spiced pumpkin & sweet potato bake with pickled onion & haloumi 106
Harissa 104

I

icings
Cream cheese icing 216
Lemon icing 270
Marshmallow icing 218

J

jamon
Broad beans & peas with jamon & mint 97
Jamon with rockmelon, mint & sherry vinegar jelly 248

K

kale
Celeriac, apple & kale slaw with smoked almonds & dehydrated anchovies 79
Chicken, kale & mushroom pie 156
Kale, banana & coconut smoothie 17

L

lamb
Greek lamb shoulder with yoghurt, cucumber & mint 170
Lamb shanks braised with beer, honey & oregano 173
lemon
Avgolemono 63
Citrus-cured ocean trout gravlax 255
Lemon icing 270
Lemon semifreddo with blackberries & lemon syrup 200
Orecchiette with tuna, spinach, mascarpone & lemon 120
Pan-fried garfish with taramasalata & soused cucumber, dill & mint salad 136
Tuna patties 132
lentils
Chicken, olive, lentil & radicchio salad 154
Spiced lentil & potato soup 69

M

Maple glaze 222
Marinated olives with orange, cinnamon & chilli 34
Marshmallow icing 218
Martini mess 211
meat
Pork & beef meatloaf with haloumi, pistachios and pomegranate molasses 174
Rigatoni bolognese with peas & basil 126
see also beef; lamb; pork
Meringue 238
Mini eclairs with chocolate cream & peanut & cashew brittle 235
Mixed leaf & herb salad with simple French vinaigrette 74
The mr. wolf chicken schnitzel & slaw 160
Muesli, toasted 14
Muffins, carrot, pineapple & walnut, with cream cheese icing 216
mushrooms
Barbecued minute steak with Asian mushroom dressing 180
Barley 'risotto' with pine mushrooms & pancetta 112
Braised chicken with white wine, Swiss brown mushrooms, pancetta & thyme 159
Chicken, kale & mushroom pie 156
Crispy prawn, crab & shiitake cigar rolls 246
Grilled mushrooms with haloumi, currants, tahini & mint 20
Roast duck, mushroom & coriander rice paper rolls 50
Mustard cream dressing 37
My go-to tuna salad 88

N

noodles
Chicken vermicelli salad with young coconut, Asian herbs & nuoc cham 94
Cold soba noodles with avocado, bean sprouts, soy, ginger & sesame 92
Egg noodles with shredded beef, Thai basil & sesame 179
Nuoc cham 94

O

octopus
    Pickled baby octopus with red wine, tomato & oregano 38
Odette's coconut roughs 228
olives
    Fennel, orange, currant & olive salad 85
    Focaccia with red onion, rosemary, olives & chilli 44
    Green olive salad 186
    Marinated olives with orange, cinnamon & chilli 34
    Tuna salad with cucumber, tomato, beetroot, radish & olives 91
orange
    Fennel, orange, currant & olive salad 85
    Marinated olives with orange, cinnamon & chilli 34
    Ratatouille 109
Orecchiette with tuna, spinach, mascarpone & lemon 120
Orzo with prawns & fennel 123

P

Pan-fried garfish with taramasalata & soused cucumber, dill & mint salad 136
Pan-fried poussin with Bois Boudran dressing 150
Pan-fried salmon with zucchini flowers, fried zucchini, chilli & mint 142
Pan-roasted snapper with garlic & bay 144
parsnip
    Celeriac & parsnip puree 185
    Pecan, parsnip, apple & maple syrup cake 222
    Roasted cauliflower & parsnip with cumin, chilli & parmesan 98
pasta
    Golden baked pasta with cauliflower & cheese 118
    Orecchiette with tuna, spinach, mascarpone & lemon 120
    Orzo with prawns & fennel 123
    Pasta e fagioli 70
    Pennette with smoked trout, crème fraîche, spinach & pancetta 124
    Rigatoni bolognese with peas & basil 126
    Spaghetti with spinach, currants, pine nuts, chilli & mint 117
pastry
    Choux pastry 235
    Sweet pastry 206
Pavlova with pineapple, pink peppercorns & citrus curd 266
Peach & pear tarts, roasted, with vanilla & thyme 208
Peanut & cashew brittle with Sichuan pepper & chilli 236
Peanut butter & banana ice cream 199
pear
    Pear, almond & chocolate cake 224
    Roasted peach & pear tarts with vanilla & thyme 208
peas
    Broad beans & peas with jamon & mint 97
    Curried rice with egg, seared salmon, peas & spring onion 138
    Rigatoni bolognese with peas & basil 126
Pecan, parsnip, apple & maple syrup cake 222
Pennette with smoked trout, crème fraîche, spinach & pancetta 124
Persillade 185
Pickled baby octopus with red wine, tomato & oregano 38
pineapple
    Carrot, pineapple & walnut muffins with cream cheese icing 216
    Pavlova with pineapple, pink peppercorns & citrus curd 266
Pita bread 42
Porchetta with rye, apple, prune & sage stuffing 264
pork
    Porchetta with rye, apple, prune & sage stuffing 264
    Pork & beef meatloaf with haloumi, pistachios and pomegranate molasses 174
    Spiced pork fillet with roasted cherry & apple chutney 260
potato
    Baked blue-eye & prawn parcels with potato, fennel & chermoula 141
    Dauphinoise 191
    Potato chip tortilla with sriracha mayonnaise 47
    Spiced lentil & potato soup 69
    Spinach, pea & potato soup 60
    Tuna patties 132
    Vinaigrette potato salad with shredded cabbage, caraway & lemon 76
    Vinaigrette potatoes with cornichons, crème fraîche, fried eggs & corned beef 30
prawns *see* seafood
Pressed chicken & prune terrine with apple, celery & watercress 37
Prosecco jelly with grapes, whipped ricotta & crushed amaretti biscuits 196
prunes
    Cider-braised smoked bacon with apples & prunes 168
    Pressed chicken & prune terrine with apple, celery & watercress 37
    Prune & apple stuffing 264
pumpkin
    Roast pumpkin soup with Thai flavours & young coconut 66
    Spiced pumpkin & sweet potato bake with pickled onion & haloumi 106

Q

quinoa
    Beetroot, quinoa & spinach salad with haloumi, sultanas & dill 82

R

Raspberry sherbet marshmallows 243
Ratatouille 109
Red velvet cupcakes with marshmallow icing 218
Red-wine braised beef cheeks with celeriac & parsnip puree 135
rice
    'Arroz campero' with prawns, calamari & mussels 114
    Baked chicken with spiced rice, cranberries & dill 162
    Curried rice with egg, seared salmon, peas & spring onion 138
    Rice paper rolls, roast duck, mushroom & coriander 50
    Rigatoni bolognese with peas & basil 126
    Roasted beetroot, cinnamon & pomegranate dip 41
    Russian salad with prawns, crab & salmon caviar 256

S

salads
    Beetroot, quinoa & spinach salad with haloumi, sultanas & dill 82
    Butter lettuce, tomato, avocado, mozzarella & pickled jalapeño salad 86
    Celeriac, apple & kale slaw with smoked almonds & dehydrated anchovies 79
    Chicken, olive, lentil & radicchio salad 154
    Chicken vermicelli salad with young coconut, Asian herbs & nuoc cham 94
    Egg & bacon salad with curly endive, Jerusalem artichoke, shallots & cornichons 80
    Fennel, orange, currant & olive salad 85

    Green olive salad 186
    Mixed leaf & herb salad with simple French vinaigrette 74
    My go-to tuna salad 88
    Russian salad with prawns, crab & salmon caviar 256
    Slaw 160
    Tuna salad with cucumber, tomato, beetroot, radish & olives 91
    Vinaigrette potato salad with shredded cabbage, caraway & lemon 76
    Yoghurt, cucumber & mint salad 170
    satay, Balinese chicken 153
sauces
    Coconut–hoisin dipping sauce 50
    Ginger–soy dipping sauce 48
    see also dressings
Scrambled curried tofu with spinach & peas 24
seafood
    'Arroz campero' with prawns, calamari & mussels 114
    Baked blue-eye & prawn parcels with potato, fennel & chermoula 141
    Barbecued flathead sandwich with iceberg, coriander & sumac aioli 135
    Chicken, prawn & shiitake pot-sticker dumplings 48
    Citrus-cured ocean trout gravlax 255
    Crispy prawn, crab & shiitake cigar rolls 246
    Curried rice with egg, seared salmon, peas & spring onion 138
    Grilled calamari & prawns with tomato, chilli, parsley, mint & moghrabieh 130
    My go-to tuna salad 88
    Orecchiette with tuna, spinach, mascarpone & lemon 120
    Orzo with prawns & fennel 123
    Pan-fried garfish with taramasalata & soused cucumber, dill & mint salad 136
    Pan-fried salmon with zucchini flowers, fried zucchini, chilli & mint 142
    Pan-roasted snapper with garlic & bay 144
    Pennette with smoked trout, crème fraîche, spinach & pancetta 124
    Pickled baby octopus with red wine, tomato & oregano 38
    Prawn baguette with minted cabbage & sumac 53
    Russian salad with prawns, crab & salmon caviar 256
    Tuna patties 132
    Tuna salad with cucumber, tomato, beetroot, radish & olives 91

Seared eye fillet with beetroot, goat's cheese, brown butter, cinnamon & sage 188
Seared rump steak with green chilli & anchovy mayonnaise & green olive salad 186
Shakshuka 23
Smoothie, kale, banana & coconut 17
soup
    Avgolemono 63
    Gazpacho rodriguez 58
    Pasta e fagioli 70
    Roast pumpkin soup with Thai flavours & young coconut 66
    Spiced lentil & potato soup 69
    Spiced tomato & chilli soup with smoked bacon 64
    Spinach, pea & potato soup 60
Spaghetti with spinach, currants, pine nuts, chilli & mint 117
Spiced apricot compote with orange blossom labna 12
Spiced lentil & potato soup 69
Spiced pork fillet with roasted cherry & apple chutney 260
Spiced pumpkin & sweet potato bake with pickled onion & haloumi 106
Spiced spinach, yoghurt & pine nut dip 41
Spiced tomato & chilli soup with smoked bacon 64
spinach
    Beetroot, quinoa & spinach salad with haloumi, sultanas & dill 82
    Filo pie with greens, ricotta & pumpkin seeds 54
    Orecchiette with tuna, spinach, mascarpone & lemon 120
    Pennette with smoked trout, crème fraîche, spinach & pancetta 124
    Scrambled curried tofu with spinach & peas 24
    Spaghetti with spinach, currants, pine nuts, chilli & mint 117
    Spiced spinach, yoghurt & pine nut dip 41
    Spinach, pea & potato soup 60
Sriracha mayonnaise 47
Stella's gingerbread star cookies 270
Sticky semolina cake with almonds, pistachios & orange blossom water 221
Strawberry trifle 269
stuffing
    for festive chicken 259
    prune & apple 264

T
Toasted muesli 14
Toffeed figs with chocolate pastry cream 194
tofu
    Scrambled curried tofu with spinach & peas 24
tomatoes
    Gazpacho rodriguez 58
    Orzo with prawns & fennel 123
    Pickled baby octopus with red wine, tomato & oregano 38
    Shakshuka 23
    Spiced tomato & chilli soup with smoked bacon 64
Tropicana rocky road 241
tuna
    My go-to tuna salad 88
    Orecchiette with tuna, spinach, mascarpone & lemon 120
    Tuna patties 132
    Tuna salad with cucumber, tomato, beetroot, radish & olives 91

V
Vanilla custard 269
vegetables
    Pasta e fagioli 70
    Ratatouille 109
    Vinaigrette potato salad with shredded cabbage, caraway & lemon 76
    Vinaigrette potatoes with cornichons, crème fraîche, fried eggs & corned beef 30

Y
yoghurt
    Grilled eggplant with tahini & yoghurt dressing, pomegranate, chilli & mint 100
    Spiced apricot compote with orange blossom labna 12
    Spiced spinach, yoghurt & pine nut dip 41
    Yoghurt, cucumber & mint salad 170

Z
zucchini
    Pan-fried salmon with zucchini flowers, fried zucchini, chilli & mint 142

A PLUM BOOK

First published in 2014 by
Pan Macmillan Australia Pty Limited
Level 25, 1 Market Street
Sydney NSW 2000, Australia

Level 1, 15-19 Claremont Street
South Yarra, Victoria 3141, Australia

Text copyright © Karen Martini 2014
Photography copyright © John Laurie 2014

The moral right of the author has been asserted.

Photography by John Laurie
Design by Allison Colpoys
Styling by Caroline Velik
Edited by Marcus Ellis
Typeset by Pauline Haas
Index by Jo Rudd
Colour reproduction by Splitting Image Colour Studio
Printed and bound in China by 1010 Printing International Limited

A CIP catalogue record for this book is available from the National Library of Australia.

All rights reserved. No part of this book may be reproduced or transmitted by any person or entity (including Google, Amazon or similar organisations), in any form or by any means, electronic or mechanical, including photocopying, recording, scanning or by any information storage and retrieval system, without prior permission in writing from the publisher.

10 9 8 7 6 5 4 3 2 1